Children and Parents Enjoying Reading

Parents and the Literacy Hour
A Teacher's Guide

Peter Branston and Mark Provis

David Fulton Publishers Ltd
Ormond House, 26–27 Boswell Street, London WC1N 3JD

First published in Great Britain by David Fulton Publishers 1999

British Library Cataloguing in Publication Data
A catalogue record for this book is available from the British Library

ISBN 1–85346–557–7

Typeset by Kate Williams, Abergavenny
Printed in Great Britain by The Cromwell Press Ltd, Trowbridge, Wilts.

Contents

To all children learning to read — we hope this book helps

Acknowledgements

The authors gratefully acknowledge the help of school staff in South Wales who have assisted in the production and testing of the materials in this book, particularly Gendros Primary School, Craigfelin Primary School, Hafod Primary Shool, St Thomas's Primary School, Godre'rgraig Primary School, Terrace Road Primary School and Trallwn Infant and Junior Schools. Staff at Perivale Primary, in the London Borough of Ealing, have been very helpful in refining and updating the Caper materials.

Particular acknowledgement should be made to Phil Andrew who helped to shape the original Caper idea and to Lynda Edwards for her enthusiastic support right from the start.

Finally, the authors and publishers would like to thank the following for providing illustrations for the book: Tony Hinwood of the Hinwood Library of Ideas, David Letissier of Graphic Books Ltd and Chartwell Illustrators Ltd.

Peter Branston and Mark Provis
October 1998

CHAPTER 1
Introduction

This book has been written for teachers who would like to foster collaborative reading between children and parents. All schools involve parents in one way or another in supporting reading, but 'involvement' is a term which bears a range of interpretations. The book offers in precise detail the requirements of a successful home–school reading scheme from the initial discussion stages right through to the evaluation of the scheme's effects. This step-by-step guide to a successful parent–school partnership makes an essential contribution to any school's literacy plan.

Children and parents enjoying reading makes such an attractive acronym, *CAPER*, that the term has been used to describe the scheme throughout. Schools using the scheme have made it their own by thinking up their own name, for example *PACER* or *Reading just for fun*.

The essential Caper kit detailed in the book includes:

- invitations to parents to meetings in school;
- two model talks for teachers for use at parents' meetings;
- a handout for parents, highlighting the main points made in the meeting;
- two parent questionnaires to help to provide feedback to your school's project;
- children's attitude scales;
- the 'parent workshop' materials;
- the 'clinic pack' for extended work with individual parents and their children;
- guidelines for schools wishing to develop volunteer parent listening groups.

The scheme recognises that the majority of parents are already involved in helping with their children's reading. Research consistently suggests that 60% of parents give help at some time. Equally, it recognises that, notwithstanding media reports to the contrary, the vast majority of children successfully learn to read. The scheme is not, then, predicated on the belief that parents are not providing support or that reading standards are falling. Our research and experience in a Local Education Authority of a large county has been that, apart from a blip in the late 1980s, reading standards have risen consistently in schools over the past two decades. Where there has been a decline it has been due to an increase in poor attainers rather than to a decline overall; the highest attainers have done as well as ever (Lake 1992).

Caper bases itself, rather, on the following assumptions:

- The first of these is that many parents give the 'wrong' kind of help, often based on their own experience of learning to read in schools-experience which is now largely out of date. Parents need guidance, which this scheme provides, on more effective ways of helping and through the workshops and clinics an understanding of the reading process and of how children learn.

- Learning to read can often be seen as a classroom competition and Caper helps to counter that view by reassuring parents that they are not expected to teach their child to read but rather to facilitate reading by showing the fun to be had from it. A surprising number of parents and children bear witness to the stress of 'reading together'. To these parents the central theme of Caper, which is how parents and children can enjoy reading together, comes as a welcome relief.
- Thirdly, it is our experience that, although parents, in the main, support their children's reading at home, the help given is often spasmodic and unsystematic. Advice to parents in the Caper scheme is to read with their children for not more than 20 minutes at a specified time each day. Built into the scheme is a simple method of monitoring this activity through the Daily Comment Booklet reproduced at the end of this book (pp. 114–18).
- The Caper programme is based firmly on the assumption that the best way of fostering any activity is through enjoyment. Teachers will be only too aware that teaching children the technical skills of reading is relatively straightforward. Unfortunately, too many children appear unable to sustain a reading habit once the basic skills have been mastered. Caper emphasises the need to sustain the primary association between reading and pleasure throughout that period when the child is acquiring technical literacy skills. Teachers and parents know that the trick is not to teach children how to read, but how to access the intrinsic pleasure of reading. Unfortunately, the message too often is that reading is a tool for some other purpose.

  The competition between reading and other media is intense. Children are bombarded with interesting and exciting things to do – hence the urgency in helping and encouraging children to become self-motivated readers (and what stronger motivator is there than pleasure?)
- A central tenet of the scheme is that, to achieve self-motivated reading, children must from the outset be treated *as* readers. Their opinions must be sought and respected. They should be helped to develop control over what they read in the same way that adults do. They need to be shown what is on offer and to be encouraged to explore their own interests, tastes and choice.

In monitoring children's reading, teachers must have regard to the response that children make to texts and not merely to the number of pages that a child reads or to narrow reading ages. Parents take their cue from teachers. The reading card in a book, which has the page number that the child has read up to, gives a clear message that learning to read is a quantitative task rather than a qualitative experience. Children are far more likely to become effective and committed readers if invited to join the 'readers' club' (Smith 1986). Guidance to parents, therefore, should encourage them to explore story, meaning and intent. Learning to read is much more than a matter of technical pedagogy and committing children to reading requires an appreciation of the link between the 'story' and deeper human motivations and desires (Bettleheim and Zelan 1982; Tucker 1984).

The Caper scheme aims to maintain commitment by treating all children as readers, by being sensitive to issues of self-esteem and by having a clear operational definition of what is meant by reading. It does this by:

- stressing first enjoyment and only later gains in reading age;
- defining a successful joint reading experience at home as one where two or more people

make meaning using text;
- ensuring that parents are enabled to provide systematic and sustained support to their child's growing literacy development;
- fostering an approach that secures success even for the least able reader;
- treating children as readers from the outset.

The challenge for teachers in developing a successful partnership with parents is to help them to understand that the reaction or response that a child has to a book is more important than the number of pages read.

The Caper scheme makes the point firmly that teachers, with their special training, will be engaged in teaching children to read and developing the skills required, for instance, to understand instructional texts. Parents are seen as collaborating with the school by providing the essential individual complementary support which enables children to practise and build upon the lessons in the Literacy Hour.

Caper provides the detail of what such collaboration looks like at its best and the means of achieving it. With its stress on books as *fun,* Caper engages parents' interest and enthusiasm and powerfully reinforces a positive commitment by children to reading.

Parents and the Literacy Hour

The National Literacy Strategy

The National Literacy Strategy will begin to be implemented in primary schools in September 1998. Its key literacy target is that, by the year 2002, 80% of 11-year-olds will reach 'Level 4 or above in the Key Stage 2 National Curriculum English tests'.

In 1997, 63% of 11-year-olds in state-funded primary schools in England and Wales achieved Level 4 or above in the English tests (Department for Education and Employment 1997). The Government's target is to increase this to 80% by 2002.

For the first time, parents are fully acknowledged as crucial partners in this process and, for this partnership between home and school to work properly, everyone needs to have a clear understanding of the Government's education framework and the language used, starting with the National Curriculum.

The National Curriculum

Teachers may need to remind parents how the National Curriculum is organised. Table 1.1 may help.

Table 1.1 Organisation of the National Curriculum

Year group	Reception	1	2	3	4	5	6	7	8	9	10	11
Age of pupils at the end of the year		5	6	7	8	9	10	11	12	13	14	15	16
Key Stage	Key Stage 1			Key Stage 2				Key Stage 3			Key Stage 4	

- Each National Curriculum subject has to be taught in 4 Key Stages 1–4 which accord with pupils' ages.
- Standards have been set in each subject for pupils aged from 5 to 14. For most of these subjects standards range from Level 1 to Level 8.
- As children become older and learn more they move through the levels. At 7, most children are expected to achieve Level 2. Most 11-year-olds are expected to achieve Level 4 and most 14-year-olds are expected to achieve Level 5 or 6. It is recognised, of course, that all children develop at different rates and that some children will be above and some below these specified levels.

In terms of reading, at Level 4, the requirement is that (Department for Education 1995):

- 'In responding to a range of texts, pupils show understanding of significant ideas, themes, events and characters, beginning to use inference and deduction.
- They refer to the text when explaining their views.
- They locate and use ideas and information.'

The Literacy Hour

The National Literacy Strategy – Framework for Teaching (Department for Education and Employment, 1998b) sets out the teaching objectives to enable children aged 5–11 to become fully literate. It also gives guidance on the 'National Literacy Hour' that should take place in every classroom each day.

To have true partnership, parents need to understand the literacy strategy and how it is being implemented in school. They are likely to have heard of the Literacy Hour through school. It would be helpful to explain this to them as part of their introduction to Caper.

In discussion on an individual basis and in groups, parents need to understand the key features of the Literacy Hour (Figure 1.1).

Therefore, parents should be made aware that:

- There is one full hour's literacy instruction in class each day.
- Work during the literacy hour is organised at three levels: firstly, the text level, where children will be looking at a passage of writing; secondly, the sentence level, where they will be looking at sentences; thirdly, the word level, where children will look at individual words.
- Each of these is addressed during the hour and the work is delivered to the class as a whole.
- While the whole class are working on an independent reading or writing task the teacher works with a group of children (at least one group for 5- to 7-year-olds and at least two for 8- to 11-year-olds) for a set time during the hour.

The parents' role

The National Literacy Hour represents a significant shift away from working with children on an individual basis, towards whole-class and group teaching. Inevitably the time available to hear children read on a regular and individual basis is reduced.

Within the Literacy Hour the class teacher works with groups, and hearing children read is acknowledged increasingly as a task for parents who are, therefore, critical to the strategy's success.

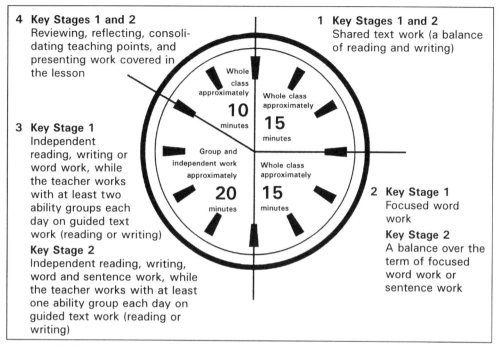

4 Key Stages 1 and 2
Reviewing, reflecting, consolidating teaching points, and presenting work covered in the lesson

3 Key Stage 1
Independent reading, writing or word work, while the teacher works with at least two ability groups each day on guided text work (reading or writing)

Key Stage 2
Independent reading, writing, word and sentence work, while the teacher works with at least one ability group each day on guided text work (reading or writing)

Whole class approximately
10 minutes

Group and independent work approximately
20 minutes

Whole class approximately
15 minutes

Whole class approximately
15 minutes

1 Key Stages 1 and 2
Shared text work (a balance of reading and writing)

2 Key Stage 1
Focused word work

Key Stage 2
A balance over the term of focused word work or sentence work

Figure 1.1 The structure of the Literacy Hour

To secure and sustain the reading partnership, the Government has proposed a fourfold framework in which parents will be (Department for Education and Employment 1998c):

1. informed about the strategy through displays, leaflets, meetings and offered the opportunity of observing the Literacy Hour;
2. involved at home, helping with reading and writing and sharing targets and records;
3. involved in school by helping during the Literacy Hour and with other activities;
4. supported in the form of workshops and training courses.

Involving parents should not be left to the efforts of individual class teachers. It is our view and one advocated by the Government that senior management in schools and local education authorities act together to introduce and extend 'the involvement of parents and the community' (Department for Education and Employment 1998a) (Figure 1.2).

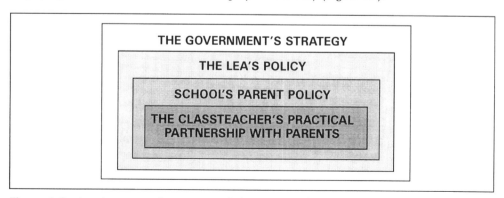

THE GOVERNMENT'S STRATEGY

THE LEA'S POLICY

SCHOOL'S PARENT POLICY

THE CLASSTEACHER'S PRACTICAL PARTNERSHIP WITH PARENTS

Figure 1.2 Involvement of parents and the community

How Caper fits into the picture

If the Government's target is the destination, the National Literacy Strategy is the vehicle and Caper improves its performance! Parents are crucial to the school's reading achievement and the Caper scheme harnesses that support effectively and to the full. The scheme encourages schools to work with parents in a far more structured, sustained and consistent manner than most normally do. Every school will have a literacy coordinator and that person's role must encompass the parent dimension.

Home–school agreements

The White Paper *Excellence in Schools* announced the Government's intention to introduce home–school agreements, which has been enacted in the School Standards and Framework Act 1998. The agreement is a statement which explains:

- the school's aims and values;
- its responsibilities towards its pupils;
- the responsibilities of the parents;
- what the school expects of its pupils.

The agreement provides a canvas against which, hopefully, the home–school reading project can flourish.

What teachers have said about the scheme

Committed teachers overwhelmingly subscribe to the effectiveness of home–school reading schemes. Teachers' responses to the Caper scheme have been recorded using critical incident diaries in which significant events are noted. A review of this record reveals very strong positive endorsement of the approach (Welsh Office 1987; Branston 1996). Teachers show their enthusiasm in the way that they extend the project beyond its original objectives. This has included displays, competitions, exhibitions in community venues and further links with the community. Extended activities at home for parents and children have been devised and visits to school set up for poets and authors. Closer links have been built up between school and parents, and parents have volunteered to come into school to act as reading helpers.

The special feature of the Caper scheme, 'the parent workshops' and 'parent clinics' are seen by teachers to have particular value. The workshops aim to provide parents with further insight into the reading process and are an opportunity for parents to let the school know how their child is progressing. The clinics are a one-to-one opportunity for teachers to observe how parents are reading with their child. Some schools offer clinic sessions to all parents, while other schools use the clinics to target parents where the home reading sessions are faltering. In our experience all parents benefit from individual guidance.

Many teachers have pointed out that in applying the clinic advice their own understanding of children's reading development has deepened. For example, one teacher saw a parent discouraging her child from asking questions as they read a story together. The teacher notes (Welsh Office 1987): 'Following her comments I questioned my own approach. We, too, tend to discourage interruption'.

The diverse response in schools shows that the scheme realises and harnesses the energy of parents in ways which are often surprising.

Schools participating in the scheme report significant gains in terms of (Andrew and Provis 1983; Curran 1985; Branston 1996):

- increased awareness of books as a source of pleasure by children;
- vastly increased book usage by children.
- a readiness among even the youngest children to use the language of books-author, title, illustrator and so on;
- increased parental involvement and support for a range of school activities;
- gains in children's reading ages that reflected the reported level of their parents' involvement.

The emphasis of Caper lies firmly in making reading at home a regular and *enjoyable* leisure activity. There are no 'pages set' and children are free to select the book of their choice from the class book stock. The success of the project hinges on good supportive adult listening to make reading 'fun'. Caper places great emphasis on the best ways of helping, which have been found invaluable by parents and teachers.

Setting out the aims of the Caper scheme

The project should be set within the school's policy for parents. Schools need to be clear about the potential of parental involvement in many aspects of school life. This will ensure that Caper harmonises with the other elements of partnership that the school is striving for.

Caper is designed as a whole-school scheme. As such it should be introduced to all staff, even though, initially, it is vital to trial the scheme in one or two classes in its first year. The reason for this graduated approach is that schools will understand the resource demands in terms of books and teacher time more clearly when, and if, a decision is taken to extend the scheme to other classes.

Aims

- The setting of aims is crucial, as a proper evaluation of the scheme's effect can only be made when outcomes are set against intentions. Clear objectives and the dates by which they will be achieved help to keep the project on target. On the other hand there are many unexpected gains from the scheme and these should be included in our evaluation of its success.

The tone of the project is set by the language used by teachers to describe it. One school's aims were generated using words such as *promote, foster, develop* and *extend*, which are all about pointing the project in the right direction:

- to *promote* the reading levels of children in school;
- to *foster* positive attitudes towards reading;

- to *develop* positive parental attitudes towards school;
- to *extend* parents' and teachers' knowledge and experience of good literature for children;
- to *strengthen* links between home and school;
- to *increase* awareness of the essential parental contribution to the learning process;
- to *develop* the connections between the reading process and other curricular areas, e.g. creative writing.

Conviction in the potential of the project is conveyed to everybody by such positive language. The confidence that you can bring to your interaction with parents is critical in sustaining their commitment.

Defining your commitment

A practical commitment by senior management is essential. Schools where the project is planned by the management team and supported by a 'project manager', who might be the literacy coordinator, have reported the greatest success.

The project manager's role would include reporting the project regularly to school governors, ensuring materials and books are available for classroom schemes to operate effectively, feeding back to class teachers not involved in the scheme start-up, helping to promote 'maintenance' activities and helping to sustain teachers', parents' and children's belief in the project.

Having agreed upon the aims of the project, schools need to plan how to run the scheme. A suggested starting point is for staff to agree on the time and resources which they can commit to the scheme and then to set out their expectations of parents and pupils. This defines the scope and scale of the plan of action. In our experience such planning enables schools to manage the project and to respond flexibly to the unforeseen opportunities that occur.

One school's commitment for teachers, parents and children is shown in Figure 1.3.

The Caper calendar — the action plan

Preparation for the scheme needs to start a term in advance. There are important things to do, especially making sure that the project is supported fully by staff and that the required commitment is there. Books in the right quantity and quality need to be available to those classes intending to begin the scheme. This is the opportunity to undertake an audit of suitable books.

There are many reasons for suggesting a September start for your home–school reading project. Children are more prepared to read at home as the nights become darker and they are not playing outside as much. By the same token the summer evenings are not really the most popular and therefore not the best time for reading with your mother or father, however skilled. Caper, therefore, runs for two and a half terms from September ending with a triumphant flourish half-way through the summer term and not with a whimper at the end of July.

Schools will want to plan to meet the needs of children whose reading development is not progressing. It is well known that the long summer break interrupts their support and their reading regresses. Project leaders and schools' senior management should link with the local education authority to secure placement for these pupils on summer literacy schemes.

As teachers our commitment is:

- to share a belief in the potential of the home–school reading project;
- to present the scheme as fun and not homework;
- to adjust classroom routines to accommodate the project;
- to maintain the home–school link through the comment booklet
- to help to ensure that a fresh supply of good literature for children is always available

We would expect parents:

- to read with their children each evening for not more than 20 minutes
- to fill in an appropriate comment about their children's reading every day
- to return the comment booklet each day to school

We expect our children:

- to read every day with their parents
- to take care of the books that they take home

Figure 1.3 One school's commitment for teachers, parents and children

All the materials mentioned in the Caper calendar (Figure 1.4) are explained in fuller detail later in the text and examples given where appropriate.

At the end of the year, plans need to be made for the following September. It is essential to secure the commitment of those teachers who are taking on pupils already in the project. They may be apprehensive, particularly if they are engaging in a parent partnership for the first time. The second year of the project may be more challenging as parent skills and expectation will have risen.

Parents will have been asked whether they want the scheme to continue. Most do. In year two there will be a clearer picture of the resources that the scheme requires. The key resource will be a new supply of interesting books.

SUMMER TERM

May	Decide to mount a scheme in school the following academic year.
June	Meet with staff to outline and gauge support for scheme. Draw up aims and action plan. Decide on the form the evaluation will take.
July	Select target classes and audit necessary resources, ensuring, in particular, that children's books are available in sufficient number and quality.

AUTUMN TERM

Within 2 weeks	Prepare Daily Comment Booklets. Prepare Guidance Booklets. Hold an evening meeting for parents.
By the end of September	Present Workshop 1.
After half-term	Issue Questionnaire 1.
By mid-November	Present Workshop 2. Organise volunteer listening groups. Plan training for this group.
By early December	Print new Daily Comment Booklets. Plan newsletter. Arrange librarian's visit to school.

SPRING TERM

At the start of term	Issue new Daily Comment Booklets.
End of week 2	Send Newsletter to parents.
By mid-February	Present Workshop 3.
By half-term	Visit to school by librarians.
After half-term	Offer individual clinic sessions.
By the end of February	Issue Questionnaire 2.
By the end of term	Present Workshop 4. Organise library visits for next term. Plan newsletter. Print new Daily Comment Booklets.

SUMMER TERM

At the start of term	Issue new Daily Comment Booklets.
End of week 2	Send Newsletter to parents.
Up to half term	Mount third series of individual clinic sessions.
During week 5	Mount Workshop 5. Plan closing Newsletter.
At some point	Organise class visit to local library.
Half-term	Newsletter to parents.
After half-term	Evaluate the project. Refine its design. Plan for next year. Make links with the Summer Literacy Scheme.

Figure 1.4 The Caper calendar

Questions that teachers will want answered

Does Caper work?

The success of parental involvement in reading projects has been widely reported, for example, by Friend (1983), by Bastiani (1993), by Topping and Wolfendale (1985) and by Wolfendale and Topping (1996).

Caper very definitely does work. It gives parents the assurance that they are helping their children constructively in their reading. It provides children with an extensive and early experience of good literature; it encourages the use of the language of books and fosters a positive commitment to reading. Caper persuades even the most reluctant reader that literacy is an attainable goal. Teachers involved in the scheme will find that, in explaining to parents how they contribute to the scheme and through the Caper clinics and workshops, they will themselves become more sensitive to the processes of learning to read. Their understanding and knowledge of pupils are broadened as, through their contact with parents, they are made more aware of how pupils react and respond at home.

However, perhaps the greatest argument in favour of parental involvement in children's reading is that it can secure about 2 hours effective adult listening for each child each week, i.e. the equivalent of four extra full-time teacher assistants in each class.

What part do parents play in the scheme?

The part that parents play in the scheme is spelt out clearly. Advice is given to them at an initial meeting, in the Caper Guidance Booklet (p. 114), in the five parent workshops (pp. 64–87) and in the individual parent reading clinics (pp. 51–54). The bias in that advice is towards reading for meaning, minimising feelings of failure for the child (and, by implication, for the parent) and extracting the maximum fun from a book. Parents are steered firmly away from sub-skills training and the complexities of phonics. The explicit message to parents is that they are not to *teach* reading but to *demonstrate the fun* that there is to be had from it.

Where do parents help?

The scheme assumes that parents help their children at home. Daily contact is established between home and school through the Daily Comment Booklet (p. 114), which for children who are six and over is filled in daily by parents, but for younger children is completed once a week.

Schools will find that some parents are more enthusiastic than others and may wish to take a more active part in Caper. For those schools wishing to avail themselves of this extra support, the scheme suggest ways in which parents can help in school.

How much time will Caper take for the teacher?

Teachers in the scheme look through every child's Comment Booklet each day and acknowledge each parent's comment. This takes no more than 10–15 minutes for the whole class. There is a space in the booklet for the teacher to respond briefly to the parents at three-weekly intervals.

The five workshops, one each half-term, take approximately 45 minutes each. In line with the Literacy Hour they generally include an activity at text level, at sentence level and word level. They are designed to help to maintain the momentum of the scheme which the first meeting engenders.

The parent clinics run throughout the project. The information in the clinic pack guides teachers on the detailed advice which particular parents may need. The teacher observes the parent listening to his or her child reading, for not more 5–10 minutes. Overall the session lasts for not more than 20 minutes.

If resources do not allow all the activities in the scheme to be undertaken, the following form the critical core:

Initial parent meeting:	This is essential; otherwise parents will not know what is expected of them and how their contribution links in with Literacy Hour.
Comment booklet:	This is essential; providing daily feedback for the teacher.
Parent workshops:	These have proved very successful in reinforcing the Caper scheme; they add to the scheme's chances of success and are therefore strongly recommended. They help to identify, within school, helpers and will provide the added insights that parents need following the introduction of the Literacy Hour.
Clinic sessions:	These are a vital chance for parents to receive one-to-one practical advice.

What resources does Caper require?

Good literature for children
Caper cannot work without a plentiful supply of good literature for children. At this point it is enough to say that children in the Caper scheme read a phenomenal number of books.

A plentiful supply of books
A basic minimum of 50 books per class per half-term is necessary for the scheme to get off the ground and to be maintained. An important challenge of the scheme, therefore, is to beg, borrow or steal sufficient books for it to succeed. Advice is provided on the first and second of these!

A stock of individualised Comment Booklets, guidance information for parents and other Caper materials arising from the project.
All these materials are set out in the book and are free for your school to photocopy.

Will Caper interfere with the reading methods already in use in school or in class?

The short answer to this is a very firm 'No!' The stress that Caper lays on the enjoyment of reading enables it to complement any reading method in school. Advice given to parents steers them away specifically from teaching reading, an activity which rests firmly with the class teacher. Caper's base in fiction and in reading for pleasure makes it unnecessary for parents in the scheme to become involved in the intricacies of instructional reading or of sub-skills training.

Children already take home books from the class reading scheme — does Caper interfere with this?

Caper coexists quite happily with reading scheme books. A teacher may require a child to read a page or two from the class reading scheme as a homework exercise. Indeed this may sometimes be at the request of the parent. This activity can continue. The important addition is of fostering the pleasure to be gained from reading through Caper.

Will Caper work in just one classroom?

Caper is a whole-school scheme and, to succeed, it needs the full support of senior management in its design, introduction and maintenance. It is suggested that the scheme should be introduced in two classrooms in the first year. This makes it possible to plan the scheme properly, to see it through to its conclusion and to evaluate its effects fully.

A two-class start is appreciated by teachers because it enables resources to be focused in sufficient quantity. A two-class start also allows the sharing of experience and resources.

Will Caper work with any group of children?

Caper is an inclusive approach. It works with all children. The materials in Caper were originally piloted with children between the ages of 6 and 8. However, it is now working successfully with pupils up to the age of 11. It has been employed with older pupils who have experienced difficulty in learning to read. It is also being used in school in modified form with pupils of nursery and reception age, i.e. between the ages of 3 and 5.

How can the scheme be evaluated?

Teachers will wish to evaluate Caper just as they would any classroom activity and precise methods for weighing up the scheme are provided. It is important to decide on the purpose of the evaluation:

- Is it a guide to future action?
- Is Caper part of the school's drive to raise standards?
- Is it to provide evidence of the significance of parental partnership to the Governors or to the local education authority?
- Is it an aid to obtaining external additional funding?
- Could it be the basis of a research project for a member of staff?

The answer will help to shape the form that the evaluation takes but may also influence what happens in the scheme itself. Some parts of the evaluation need to occur towards the beginning and at the end of the project. Ideally, therefore, questions about the kind of evaluation that the school wishes to undertake need to be resolved at the outset.

Two sorts of measure are suggested:

- The more subjective aspects of the scheme relate to changes in attitude, which can be assessed using the children's attitude scales and the parental questionnaires.
- Objective aspects, such as changes in reading age or number of books read, are easily measured.

The 'style' of the scheme

Caper will read as very prescriptive to some teachers, who may wish to make modifications to it. Clearly it will adapt easily without loss of its central theme. In our experience, teachers have welcomed Caper's precise structuring mainly because they have relatively little experience in working systematically with parents. Addressing a group of parents is recognised as a sometimes daunting task, quite different from that of standing in front of a class of children. Thus the 'model talks' to parents, which have been employed with a great deal of success, can, if a teacher wishes, be used verbatim.

Secondly, the campaigning style of the scheme may not appeal to everyone. Our experience, however, is that illustrated headings to letters, well-designed and frequent use of graphics and a confident approach to parents help to promote an enthusiasm for the project which is an important ingredient in its success. It is essential that teachers tell parents how much they value their contribution. Parents will in turn respond to such appreciation.

Will the scheme work with parents and children for whom English is an additional language?

The Caper scheme can play a vital part in promoting the written and oral language skills of children for whom English is an additional language (EAL) or whose parents are not fluent English speakers. An essential feature of Caper is it insistence on the use of good fiction for children. Children's picture books are an excellent way to promote language skills for parents who have difficulty in reading or speaking English. The texts selected provide the necessary ingredients for language learning to occur. The 'story line' is very strong and holds the interest of child *and* adult. There is the repetition of sentence, phrase and word. There is plenty of additional information that aids textual prediction.

Consider the repetition in *We're Going on a Bear Hunt* by Michael Rosen and Helen Oxenbury, where the 'verse' appears on every other page:

> We're going on a bear hunt
> We're going to catch a big one
> What a beautiful day!
> We're not scared.

This repetition within the text and the repetition imposed by the child who insists on hearing the story read over and over again helps to develop language skills. The essential rhythm in the text links oral and written language in a way that bridges cultures. Almost all picture books contain this rhythmic repetitive language, which children and their parents love and learn from. They follow on naturally from language games, songs and nursery rhymes learnt before school.

In a recent parent workshop undertaken by one of the authors, parents from diverse cultural backgrounds were discussing Allen and Janet Ahlbergs' *Peepo* and what their home language equivalent of that word would be. Everyone recognised the peepo game and the word too was surprisingly universal. One parent read the story out loud and by the end of the book we were all chanting, 'Here's a little baby. One, two, three. Sits in his high chair. What does he see? Peepo!'

The Very Hungry Caterpillar by Eric Carle provides a text and illustrations that almost speak to you. The level of information in Eric Carle's book is so high that the story tells itself and it is not difficult to predict text or to 'cloze'.

The suitability of texts for EAL pupils will depend upon the stage that they are at in learning English and their age and interests. 'Core books', chosen because of the positive way in which race, gender and class are presented and available in multiple copies in school, are used increasingly as part of the teaching of written language. For teachers wishing to know more about core books for EAL students *Language Activities for Bi-lingual Learners* and *Language Works* make essential reading. They are available from Learning by Design, Tower Hamlets Education, English Street, London E3 4TA.

Gregory (1996) pointed out the need to examine carefully the expectations that parents in multi-ethnic areas may have of schools. She suggested that some parents may view methods in school as insufficiently directive and that successful home–school literacy projects need to take this on board. In her study, Gregory investigated the educational practices in the Arabic and Bengali classes that children attended outside school and noted teaching patterns very different from those in school. These methods were incorporated into the programme that she and her co-workers devised (Gregory 1996): 'The main advantage of our approach is that we were able to build up a picture of the child and family's literacy world before beginning to design a home–school reading programme.'

The Caper workshops are an ideal forum for schools to explore alternative views that parents may hold on the teaching process and to adapt the strategies for parental support that the school is suggesting.

CHAPTER 2
Some research findings

Reading projects and the growing emphasis on literacy

Topping and Wolfendale (1985) give a detailed account of early work in home–school part-
nerships, inspired largely by the Plowden Report and by the pioneering work of Hewison
(1979) and Tizard *et al.* (1982). This includes Hackney PACT (Hancock and Gale 1992),
pause, prompt and praise (Glynn *et al.* 1979) and paired reading (Morgan 1976, Topping
and Wolfendale 1985). Caper began in South Wales with its distinctive stress upon reading
as a process rather than a set of skills to be acquired (Edwards and Branston 1979, Branston
and Provis 1984a, Branston 1988). Wolfendale and Topping (1996) described how the term
family literacy has now come to be used to describe an approach to developing reading
which involves not just the child, but the family *context*. Caper sits firmly in this tradition,
because its original focus was the family rather than the school and because of its emphasis
on working with parents in school through the workshops and clinics. The suggestions for
maintaining the scheme develop it beyond its initial literacy focus and have consistently led
to wider community activities and to broader conceptions within the school of the parental
contribution to education. Large-scale studies over time, such as those of Douglas (1964)
and Davie *et al.* (1972), have all suggested that factors in the child's home affect performance in school. This has become an established truth in the minds of many involved with
children and their education. Yet until the latter part of the 1970s no one had been able to
isolate any factor or group of factors within the home background of children that helped to
in their performance at school.

Parental support makes a big impact on children's educational progress

Teachers work with classes which may exceed thirty pupils and the time a teacher can spend
with any individual is limited. The Literacy Hour's emphasis on guided and shared reading, on
class lessons and on group work reduces opportunities for one to one support even further.
Schools developing schemes like Caper secure individual daily support for each child that reaps
a rich reward in terms of developmental gain.

Parents are asking for guidance on how best to help

The vast majority of parents would help their children in support of their education if only they were offered some advice and guidance and ongoing encouragement. Teachers cannot expect parents to ask outright for such aid. The onus is on the school to initiate an appropriate dialogue.

Schools should spell out and structure the home–school partnership

The vast majority of parents are helping their children in support of their education, but their support could be so much more effective with structured advice and guidance from school. School guidance needs to be responsive to parents' concerns.

Reading tends to be left to the mother

Support for reading at home is all too often left to the mother or other female members of the family. The reading skills of boys are generally lower than those of girls and one reason for this is that men are not reading with their children at home. Without male reading models, the activity comes to be seen as essentially female. Caper goes out of its way to target male as well as female listeners. One significant change noted in home–school schemes is that the range of people helping at home widens significantly (Welsh Office 1987).

Schools need to reassure parents regularly that their contributions are valued

Regardless of the changing climate in schools, parents can still feel uncomfortable and out of place in a school setting. Typical remarks continue to be made such as:

- 'I never had to go there as there was no trouble.'
- 'I never had any complaint and knew the school was doing its best for him.'

For many parents the idea that no news is good news is still frequently expressed, with many parents only expecting a dialogue with teachers when there is a problem. There are still parents who:

- tend to delegate all the responsibilities for their children's learning to school;
- are reluctant to attend school at any time, save by invitation;
- lack confidence in their ability to have a satisfactory discussion with the teachers and expect a one-sided conversation.

The implication is that schools need to think creatively of ways of engaging a wider group of parents (Bastiani 1993; Bastiani and Wolfendale 1996). It is this book's contention that the majority of parents are unaware of the scope or the impact that they can have on their children's school achievement. With positive and sustained guidance from school they are anxious and able to give support.

Teachers can develop negative attitudes to parents

Teacher can attribute disinterest to parents, whereas there may be many reasons for what appears to be apathy.

- Parents may be unaware of the important part that they play in their children's education.
- Parents are busy people and finding the time is difficult.

The positive attitude of the school is critical in securing this extra time against other competing demands and in maintaining the parents' input.

School is the key source of advice and guidance on educational matters

Schools tend to underestimate their accumulated expertise and knowledge on how children learn. Teachers could assist parents much more than they do in advising how to promote children's educational development. Assistance with reading is a parenting skill which parents are only too willing to exercise if they can be given the right kind of practical advice.

The key challenge for school is to maintain regular parental support

It is not enough to have a policy on parental involvement in reading and to introduce the scheme to parents at a meeting. Some schools simply lend out books and let the parents get on with it. Not surprisingly these approaches have limited success and lead to teacher pessimism about schemes in general. Maintenance activities are a vital part of any successful scheme. The Caper scheme is packed with support and maintenance activity.

'You can take a horse to water but you can't make it drink'

Most recently, in Britain, recommendations have been made on the amount of homework children should be set and the time to be spent doing it. While appreciating the importance of home study, teachers are aware of the danger of associating an activity which is essentially pleasurable with homework. There has never been any doubt that teachers have the methodology and the expertise to teach reading. The difficulty has always been one of helping children to develop and sustain a reading habit. The emphasis in the past has been about reading as a set of skills rather than as an enjoyable activity which helps us make sense of our world. A desire to read must be fostered through this enjoyment; it cannot be forced.

Beware the temptation of underestimating the parental role

In terms of time and opportunity to interact with children as individuals, the parent–child dyad is potentially more capable of providing stimulation and generating cognitive growth than the comparatively brief interludes that a teacher can give to one child. The teacher may possess the skills but cannot spend the same amount of time in contact with the individual child that the parent can. The answer lies in getting parents and teachers to recognise this situation so that its potential can be fully maximised for the benefit of the child.

Getting the most from parents

Caper gives practical guidance on approaching parents and the necessary advice to enable them to give positive support in reading development.

Parents may:

- have negative attitudes, arising from their own educational experiences;
- wrongly estimate their children's abilities (in special education this may mean underestimate);
- attribute unrealistic levels of expertise to professionals.

Caper attempts to break through these barriers to parental cooperation by:

- explaining how parents should help;
- asking for a commitment from them of just 20 minutes a day;
- sensitising parents to their children's performance;
- encouraging parents' awareness of their child's reading development.

Teachers have little training in working with parents

A survey of initial training by Atkin and Bastiani (1985) showed that over half of post-graduate certificate of education students, and one in four students on longer courses, had no preparation for work with parents. There is little sign that the situation has changed much since then. Consequently, there is a danger that many enthusiastic teachers will develop views on the potential for parental involvement in the form of received wisdom from older, more experienced colleagues whose own contact with parents has been less than fruitful. Others might recognise the promise that such contact offers and yet feel reluctant to take the initiative and to be the innovator who breaks new ground in a school.

Other approaches

The PACT project

The parents, children and teachers (PACT) scheme began in 1979 in primary schools in Hackney, an area in the East End of London. Its evangelical aim was 'to spread ideas, to find resources and to take the message to the unconverted'.

PACT recognises three crucial elements in developing a successful scheme:

- schools need to find ways of making contact with parents;
- parents need advice on how to hear children read effectively;
- the contact between parent and teacher must be maintained.

The PACT team generated such enthusiasm for the project that 34 out of 48 Hackney primary schools joined the project in its first 4 years. There are no precise rules as to how a school should initiate a PACT scheme. For schools seeking guidance there are PACT booklets and newsheets. The PACT team has published a book reporting their experience (Griffiths and Hamilton 1984). More recently PACT has continued to promote parental involvement in reading through home reading programmes and family literacy initiatives (Hancock and Gale 1992).

Pause, prompt and praise

This is a tutoring procedure which is recommended specifically for 'low-progress readers', which originated in New Zealand in 1979 and has been extensively researched since then. Tutoring requires *pausing* when the reader makes an error to allow for self-correction. The tutor then provides a *prompt* which may be a semantic clue, a syntactic clue or a phonic clue. *Praise* is then given for a corrected response. There is extensive evidence that even skilled practitioners do not listen and support children's reading using these strategies (Wheldall *et al.* 1992). Pause, prompt and praise is intended for pupils who are not progressing adequately and there is evidence that the approach is not helpful for average and above average readers (Wheldall and Glynn 1989). However, Glynn and other researchers have demonstrated that this structured approach is also helpful in developing the reading skills of reading tutors (Medcalf and Glynn 1987).

Paired reading

This is a technique for promoting children's reading which is known around the world. It is outlined later in the book, but for a full description of the 'proper method', see Topping and Wolfendale (1985).

CHAPTER 3
The Caper book stock

It is essential that a plentiful supply of books is available in the classes where Caper is introduced. Teachers who have introduced the scheme have consistently remarked on the 'voracious demand for books' (Welsh Office 1987) which the scheme generates.

"He consumes books at an enormous rate."

How many books?

A critical measure of the success of the scheme in each class is the number of books which each child reads (Provis 1983). Each class should aim to have a stock of 50 books at any one time and our experience is that these will need to be changed each half term. If you are using significantly fewer books than this the scheme is not working as well as it can. Since 50 books will be quickly read by a class of average size, books will need to be rotated between classes involved in the scheme. Hence there is a reduction in the overall resources required if more than one class in school is working with the scheme.

Table 3.1   Overall book requirement

| Year group | Number of books for: | |
	1 form entry	2 form entry
Nursery	150 (50 × 3)	200
Reception	150 (50 × 3)	200
Years 1–6	900 (150 × 6)	1200
Total	1200	1600

One idea thought up by a teacher to increase book circulation was to develop a book-sharing scheme in her class. Children bring their favourite books to school and are given an equivalent number of tickets. They then swop these tickets for books, which other children have brought to school.

Where there is a three-form entry the number of books required will not be substantially higher than this as classes share the book stock. Nevertheless, this represents a substantial resource investment and adds weight to the argument for introducing the scheme with one or two age groups at a time.

Which books are suitable?

Schools are engaged in an audit of their book stock in response to the National Literacy Project and to qualify for Government grant funding. This will help to ensure that the books available are suitable for the Caper scheme. It is important that books in the Caper scheme should resemble reading scheme books as little as possible. Caper has always been a scheme based on children's fiction and aims to develop a child's desire to read through linking reading and pleasure. This is not at all to gainsay reading schemes, which are an essential part of the reading teacher's armoury. The content of reading scheme books has improved immeasurably from the days of Janet and John, but vertical movement through the scheme continues to be regarded by parents and children as the essential motivator. The book that the child is on is a measure of his or her reading attainment and is the signifier of success for the child, parent and teacher. Reading schemes can encourage the view that children are not yet ready for 'real' books, and teachers still encounter the view among parents that children ought not to move to 'real' books until they have reached a certain reading level.

- There is also an inevitable element of competition in the Caper scheme, but there are no judgements in it about reading capability or attainment and it works equally well with children who are struggling to attain reading fluency and with 'high fliers'. Teachers leading the scheme need to 'manage' this sense of competition to ensure that the emphasis upon enjoyment is maintained for all children.
- Schools in the scheme are promoting a regular independent reading habit among children (which can change wider family reading habits). The books themselves, their covers and general appearance affect the outcome of the project. To give the project the right kind of image in children's eyes, books chosen should be up to date. Books inherited from other teachers and classes over the years and accumulated when it would have been kinder to recycle them are unlikely to give the scheme the desired image. Multiple

copies of favourite books need to be available. Popular dog-eared books need to be renewed.

The advice given to parents relates to one kind of reading, i.e. reading for pleasure. Caper books are therefore nearly always *fiction*. Non-fiction material requires quite a different range of reading strategies, which do not fit easily into the Caper model.

'Easy' or 'hard' books

The books chosen for each class will be broadly age appropriate, but teachers will be wary of trying to organise books according to their difficulty level. Some books defy this kind of categorisation.

Consider the various ways in which illustration and text work together. In some stories the relationship appears straightforward, in others it is altogether more complex. John Burningham's *Come Away from the Water, Shirley* has two stories; both are told in pictures – a death-defying adventure with pirates for Shirley and a deckchair day on the beach for her parents. In their enthusiasm for this book, children demonstrate just how well they can manage two stories told simultaneously and stories where the normal rules do not appear to apply (Lewis 1992).

Rosie's famous stroll around the farmyard before tea, in *Rosie's Walk*, by Pat Hutchins, told in one sentence of 32 words, is far from a simple story. The reader wonders:

- Does Rosie know that the fox is there?
- Surely she must?
- Why otherwise would she lead the fox such a merry dance?

All of this in 32 words!

Authors such as John Burningham, Pat Hutchins and the Ahlbergs are teaching children how to read text and pictures in books that are complex works of art, and it is only relatively recently that we have come to recognise that the books which we choose for children critically influence what they learn (Meek 1988; Kimberley *et al.* 1992). These are far from 'simple' texts.

The Caper scheme aims to develop an early habit of regular reading. This can only be done if the books used, particularly at the beginning of the project, are accessible to children, are enjoyable and provide ready success. Fluent readers will often want to return to a favourite book, a book that we might have categorised as too easy. 'Easy-to-read' fiction counters the strong sense which very many children have that reading is a chore and mainly about getting through the reading scheme and only then on to 'real' or 'library' books.

We need to challenge the view commonly held by children and their parents that 'easy' books are necessarily babyish and therefore not worth consideration. They play a vital role in hooking children onto books. This is particularly true for children who have not made a great success of reading early on and for whom reading is a technical accomplishment, rather than a primary source of meaning and pleasure.

Getting to know books

Teachers working with Caper immerse themselves in children's fiction. Everyone in the scheme finds out more about children's fiction or about those books which do and do not work with children. Children's librarians are a mine of information. They can supply book lists and may well be willing to address parent or staff groups. Teachers can make a class visit to the local library and invite parents to come too.

All schools will have copies of publishers' catalogues, for example, Heinemann Literacy Catalogue, MacDonald Young Books and Oxford Books for Children and Young Adults. It is helpful in addition to have independent advice on books that work well with children.

The Young Book Trust Library, Book House, 45 East Hill, London SW18 2QZ, is an invaluable source of information about children's books. This includes fully annotated lists of books for children according to broad age groups: beginning to read, 5–8; newly fluent readers, 6–10; adventurous readers, 12+; able readers, 10–12; books for readers, 14+. There are theme titles, e.g. bullying, and book titles for the very young.

- *The Hundred Best Books*, published by the Book Trust and available from Book House is a fully annotated guide to the best paperback books for children.
- *The Puffin Literacy Hour Book List* compiled by Wendy Cooling is available from most booksellers and provides titles of fiction and poetry organised according to the National Curriculum year and term.
- *Books for Keeps*, published six times a year, can be obtained from 6 Brightfield Road, Lee, London SE12 8QF.
- *Books for Your Children*, published four times a year, from Books for Your Children, 90 Gilhurst Road, Harborne, Birmingham B17 8PA, is a lively information magazine written mainly for parents.
- *Carousel Guide to Children's Books*, published three times yearly (March, June and October) can be obtained from 7 Carrs Lane, Birmingham B4 7TG.
- *Children's Book News*, published three times yearly, is available from the Young Book Trust (see above).
- *Signal: Approaches to Children's Books*, published three times a year, from Thimble Press, Lockwood, Station Road, South Woodchester, Stroud, Gloucestershire GL5 5EQ, is a critical review magazine.
- *Junior Paperback Catalogue* is available from Books for Students, 58–64 Berrington Road, Leamington Spa, Warwickshire CV31 1NB.
- *Letterbox Library*, published quarterly, contains suggested titles which are representative of a multi-cultural world 'from the local to the global'. It contains details of dual-language books and is available from Letterbox Library Unit 2D, Leroy House, 436 Essex Road, London N1 3QP.

Three excellent books, which deserve a place in the staff library, are:

- *Learning to Read with Picture Books* by Jill Bennett (1995, 4th edn, Thimble Press).
- *Learning to Read* by Margaret Meek (1995, 3rd edn, Bodley Head)—an extremely readable book for parents, which suggests titles for every age group, all of which are suitable for Caper.
- *Babies Need Books* by Dorothy Butler (1995, 3rd edn, Bodley Head)—an excellent book which parents and teacher will find very useful. It lists books for the age group 0–6, which should be available if Caper is introduced to nursery or reception classes.

Two more books should be mentioned:

- *Children's Literature and the Politics of Equality* by Pat Pinsent (1997, David Fulton Publishers) deals very articulately with sexist and racist issues in children's literature.

- *International Companion Encyclopaedia on Children's Literature* by Peter Hunt (1997, Routledge and Kegan Paul) is a truly magnificent reference book containing everything that you ever wished to know about children's books. It merits a place in every staff library.

CHAPTER 4

Introducing parents to Caper

The project begins with an invitation to parents to attend a meeting on 'children's reading'. The invitation, like all Caper materials, should be eye catching. Wherever possible the approach to parents should be made with humour and should differ markedly from normal routine school letters. Experience has shown that, the more stimulating the initial letter, the better the parental response.

Naturally teachers know their own schools best and may prefer to devise a letter that will strike the right chord with their parents.

The invitation is sent to those parents whose children are in the classes participating in the project.

Invitation to the parents

Letter 1 (Figure 4.1) is sent to parents to assess their initial response to a Caper meeting. Please note that *all* letters and other project materials should be individualised for your school.

If you are confident that most parents will attend a meeting, letter 1 is not needed and you should start with *letter 2* (Figure 4.2). Experience suggests that Friday evening is a poor choice for a parents' meeting. Do not forget to fill in the name of the school in the drum (letter 1) or box (letters 2 and 3).

Inevitably, some parents are unable to attend the initial meeting and a further meeting should be held just for them, using *letter 3* (Figure 4.3). This attempts to draw in those parents who did not come to the first meeting by offering a more detailed invitation.

The tear-off slip on letter 3 gives parents unable or unwilling to come to meetings the opportunity of individual interviews.

There will be a small number of parents who will not respond to these invitations. You may decide that everything possible has been done to engage these parents in the scheme and accept that some parents will choose to remain outside the project.

Experience has shown that a telephone call or a home visit can act to stimulate the interest of this reluctant group. The question of home visiting is delicate and teachers who undertake home visits will be aware of the need to ask first, through the child, whether such a visit would be welcome.

Dear

We are drumming up interest in our own parental involvement in the reading project.

If you would like to be involved with your child's reading development, please indicate below whether you would prefer to attend an afternoon or an evening meeting to hear more about the scheme.

Yours sincerely,

I would prefer to attend an $\left\{\begin{array}{l}\text{afternoon}\\\text{evening}\end{array}\right\}$ meeting.

I cannot attend a meeting on a Monday/Tuesday/Wednesday/Thursday.

Signed _____ Parent of _____

Figure 4.1   The first letter to parents – offering a choice increases attendance

Dear

We are putting out the welcome mat to parents who would like to hear what the Caper project can offer them and their child. The word 'Caper' stands for 'Children and Parents Enjoying Reading'.

If you are interested a meeting has been arranged at

on

Could you please let us know if you are able to attend?

Yours sincerely,

- -

I shall be able to attend on _____

I shall not be able to attend on _____

Signed _____   Parent of _____

Figure 4.2 The letter of invitation – requests feedback

Dear

I was so sorry that you missed the reading meeting held at the school on_____. For those parents who were unable to attend, we are holding a second meeting on_____.

The purpose of this meeting is to explain how the school teaches reading, the importance of parental help to develop children's reading and how you can best help your child when he or she gets stuck on a word.

At this meeting all parents will be given a booklet entitled *Helping Your Child to Enjoy Reading*.

Please make a special effort to attend this daytime meeting.

Yours sincerely,

- -

I shall be able to attend the meeting on _____

I would rather come another time_____

Signed _____ Parent of _____

Figure 4.3 A follow up letter for parents unable to attend first meeting

---

Checklist for the first meeting

- The preferred times for meetings are the start or the end of the school day, when some parents will be bringing or collecting their children. Evening meetings (avoid Friday) are generally well attended.

- The overhead projector and transparencies should be ready in advance.

- Sufficient copies of the Caper Guidance Booklet and the Daily Comment Booklet, reproduced in Appendices with instructions on how to assemble (pp. 113–124)

- Since reference is made in the talk to 'good literature for children', a display of this should be in evidence. An approach sometimes used is to distribute books to parents while latecomers arrive.

- An attendance record should be kept to establish who is still to be contacted. A clipboard and pen should be circulated during the meeting.

- Refreshments should be provided at either the beginning or the end of the meeting. Refreshments demonstrate the school's commitment to the project and reinforce the school's welcome to parents.

Figure 4.4   Checklist for the first meeting

The first meeting

The first meeting with a group of parents can be a considerable challenge for the teacher. The above checklist (Figure 4.4) may be helpful.

Talking with parents

Two 'model talks', given to parents at an initial meeting, have been developed over the course of the Caper project. One talk begins by treating the parent group as a mock class, an approach that assumes a reasonably informal relationship between teacher and parent. Experience suggests that this style of presentation breaks the ice and encourages greater parental participation in the meeting and subsequently the project. The second 'model talk' is recommended for use with parents of younger children (three- to five-year-olds) where the emphasis is on parents' skills of reading with, rather than listening to, children. This talk will be found in the section on Caper with nursery or reception age pupils (pp. 91–9).

Some teachers may not wish to use the talks in their present form. The talks have been included in this unashamedly prescriptive way for the following reasons:

- Teachers are unlikely to have received training in working with parents.
- Teachers have little *experience* of working with groups of parents.
- Teachers are often uncertain how to approach parents and what to say to them in groups.

Teachers and parents have responded favourably to the two 'model talks'.

By all means modify the talks or the presentations. It is important, however, to cover the main points within each.

CHAPTER 5

Model talk to parents of six- to eight-year-olds

Head teacher's introduction (5–10 minutes)

The opening 10 minutes of introduction by the head teacher or the language specialist in the school includes an outline of the school's approach to the teaching of reading through the Literacy Hour.

Caper talk – head teacher, class teacher or outside speaker – 40 minutes

A light-hearted way to introduce the Caper is to address the parents as a class. 'Right, class, settle down!'

Question session

'Hands up all those parents of children in Mrs ———'s class. Come along, quickly! This class is asleep today!

Hands up those parents who used to read to their children regularly.

   I see, most of you – good.

Hands up those parents who still read to their children regularly.

   Not quite so many.

Hands up those parents who listen to their children read at least every other day.

   Getting fewer.

Hands up those parents who talk about the pictures in the book.

   A handful.

Hands up those parents who talk about the story with their children.

Hands up those parents who quickly say the word when their children get stuck.

Hands up those parents who asked the school about their approach to reading.

Hands up those parents who have asked the school what they can best do to help their children's reading'

In practice, this elimination game should have been won by the speaker long before the end. Anyone left in the game is a saint!

The research

'We know that 60% of all parents help with their children's reading at some point in time. However, the research has shown that the most effective help that parents can give their children, and one of the most important factors in children's reading development, is for the parents to listen to their children read aloud regularly at home. The purpose of this talk is to enlist your support in listening to your children read at home and to ensure that this support is consistent with the school's approach to reading and that you and your children enjoy reading together.'

The analogy with speech

'Who taught your children to talk? How? You talked to them.

Then you listened to *their efforts* at forming speech.

Then you talked together.

This process is still going on today. Apply this to reading with your children.

Remember that, even if your children are good readers, they are still only reading with the understanding, knowledge and insight of 6- (7-) (8-)year-olds. Even very able young readers need the support and understanding of good listeners.'

How to listen to your child read

- Are you sitting comfortably? 'Sit side by side so that you can both see the book easily, ideally in a room where there are no distractions, such as a television set, or brothers and sisters.'
- Talk about the picture. 'Explore the picture on the page before your children begin to read. Ask them what is happening in the picture. You will find that they will often use the language of the book itself and in this way will begin to anticipate the meaning of the print.'
- Talk about the story. 'Never recommence a story half-way through without reviewing the story up to that point. If you ended on, say, page 26 yesterday, do not just begin again on page 27 today, but get your children to retell the story so far in their own words.'
- What happens next? 'Ask your children to predict the direction that the story will take so that they can compare their guesses with the story as the reading goes on. This tends to heighten their involvement with the text.'
- Respond to the book. 'Make your response to the difficulty level of books flexible; ask your children to read but, if the book is too difficult, be prepared to share the reading or even to read it to them. If you do the reading, make sure that your children can follow the print and that you "act" the story out with enthusiasm. Another solution is that, where the book is a little difficult for your children to read, be prepared to read the page first and then get them to read it after you. It is still reading: the reader's eyes are on the page, they are scanning the print and then saying the words. Try to remember that reading aloud is much harder than reading silently.'

- What do we do if our children get stuck? 'When children get stuck on a word, most parents ask them to 'sound it out' without realising just how difficult this is for children. Try this.'

Using the overhead projector, the speaker gets the parents to sound out the word (cat), letter by letter, as in Figure 5.1.

'Never heard of it before – this is the creature that you named: cu aa tu' (Figure 5.2).

Figure 5.1 cat

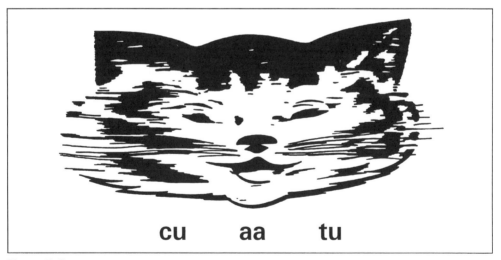

Figure 5.2 cu aa tu

'You have all stretched the letters out to the point where they do not make sense. Asking children to sound out a word is often a mistake and the teaching of these "phonic" skills is best left to the class teacher.'

If an overhead projector is not available, try the following as a group exercise.

'Sounding out is much more difficult for children than we realise. What makes it hard is that they cannot be certain of the sound value of each letter until they know what the word actually says. Someone reading with children will know the word and, therefore, the sound value of each letter. If you know the word, phonics is easy, if you do not it is very hard.'

At this point the teacher chooses a word (GEORGIE works very well) and writes its initial letter on the board. The teacher knows the word; parents do not. The teacher asks the parents to sound out the first letter. Usually parents will give a soft G, sometimes a hard G; sometimes the name rather than the sound of the letter. Encourage the class.

'Come on, you know this word. We had it yesterday!'

Add the letters one by one, asking for 'sounding out' each time. Notice how often the group attempts to guess. The points to be drawn out are:

- that even experienced readers confuse the sound and name of the letter and that we need to be consistent in our use of these terms;
- that it is difficult to guess sound values when the word is unknown;
- that a major source of irritation between learner and helper is involvement in a task together where one defines the task as 'hard', and the other as 'easy' (this is especially true where they are related, as anyone who has taught a husband or wife to drive will testify!);
- crucially for Caper, that this whole phonic exercise would have seriously interrupted the flow of the story which a child and parent were reading together;
- that sounding out is just one of the strategies which a child uses to work out unknown words.

'The key to good supportive listening help is to look at your children to see whether they are still scanning the print. If not, *say the word*.

It may be necessary for the listener to say the word two or three times in one listening session. Occasionally, it may be helpful to give the *first* sound of a word that has already been met several times in the text.'

- Perfect sense? 'You are being involved in your children's leisure reading; so you should *not* attempt to correct every small mistake, but accept those that do not affect the sense of the story. If you do this, the story will flow and your children will enjoy the experience and be prepared to repeat it.'
- When to listen? 'Ideally you should attempt to listen to your children read every day, at a time convenient to you both, for not more than 20 minutes. Little and often is the key to successful listening.'
- Praise. 'Successful listeners praise their children frequently throughout each reading session for their effort at reading.' (Many parents will wince at the mention of the red-faced table thumper who screams at the top of his or her voice, 'I told you that before!')

'It is important that the tone of the session together be positive and that you act as a supportive listener, giving words of encouragement, "good", "well done", "great", or simply sounds, "Ah ha" or "Mmmmm". Some parents find this extremely difficult, but it is crucial to successful listening. If you notice that your children start to correct their own errors, it suggests that they are thinking about the meaning of what is being read and you should adjust your listening accordingly.'

Good practice

At this point in the talk a school-made video of 'good practice' can be played to the parents to illustrate and reinforce the central points of the talk. It is an excellent learning (and often a salutary) experience for teachers to tape each other listening to children reading and to check that they can follow their own advice!

A cloze exercise

To illustrate further the points in the talk, the 'class' can be offered a cloze exercise. Such an exercise should always reflect a contemporary theme. The passage in Figure 5.3 is part of a conversation between parents overheard in the corridor one afternoon.

The parents are asked to offer the words used in the blanks. This has to be handled with some sensitivity and care must be taken not to focus on anyone.

The points to be drawn from the exercise are:

- Did you 'sound out' the missing words?
- Did you read up to the missing word and guess it?
- Did you read beyond the missing word and guess back to it?
- Did you have to use knowledge to find the word?

The exercise helps the group to generate ideas on just how children learn to read.

For weeks now the _____ have been nagging at _____ to let them _____ and see the new film of the 101 _____ . I'm so fed up with _____ that I'll _____ give in and _____ them on _____ as it's their Dad's day _____ . The _____ time we _____ to the _____ we saw a Disney _____ . They still make _____ laugh. My _____ is Snow _____ and the _____ Dwarfs. I love the _____ called Doc.

Figure 5.3 Cloze exercise

Summary of the Caper approach

The ideas raised by the talk are then reviewed by quickly running through the guidance book-let *Helping Your Child to Enjoy Reading*, which is distributed at this point. It is reproduced in the Appendices on pp. 114–117 for you to photocopy, personalising the project by adding the name of your own school in the box on the front.

What to read

The parents are told that their children will constantly have a Caper book at home. These books will not be graded, as the children will have a free choice of a book from those selected for the scheme. The parents are asked to adjust their listening strategy according to the diffi-culty level of the book. This will give their children access to any book that they wish to read.

A short reading from a book such as *Not Now Bernard* by David McKee (Anderson Press; Sparrow), or *Sheep in Wolves' Clothing* by Satoshi Kitamura (Anderson Press), or a verse from Roald Dahl's *Revolting Rhymes* (Cape; Picture Puffin), will illustrate the fun to be had from children's books, plus the need for children to have access to such stories now, whatever their ages.

If a book is too hard, then parents are asked to read it to their children. If the book seems unsuitable, it should be returned to the school. The message is that the fault lies with the book and not the child. It is stressed that the books must always be read in meaningful units and not as x pages a day.

Parents are cautioned that listening sessions are more effective if they end while interest is still high. A time of 20 minutes is more than enough. Parents who find longer sessions successful may continue with them, provided that they are not pressurising their children.

How to use the Daily Comment Booklet

This is introduced as the pivotal point of contact with the class teacher. Having committed themselves to listening to their children read, the parents are asked to make a short comment in the Daily Comment Booklet. This booklet *must* be returned to school each morning. Each child will bring the Comment Booklet home each afternoon.

The programme of clinics and workshops

The talk closes with the speaker outlining the programme of clinics and workshops. This provides the opportunity to secure the parents' commitment to attending future Caper events.

Questions and answers

Many parents take the chance to welcome the project. Some will have held off rather than conflict with the school's approach to reading. Others may relate experiences that highlight points made by the talk. Suggested answers to some questions which may be raised are given below.

Question: Is reading comics a bad thing?

Answer: Any reading material that your child enjoys should be encouraged and this includes comics.

Question: My child reads very fast. He seems to gabble at words. Is this a bad thing?

Answer: Try to slow him down if he does not understand what he reads. Asking questions about what he is reading is a good way of changing pace. A parent should take opportunities of modelling good reading.

Question: My child seems to guess a great deal. Is this a good thing?

Answer: We all 'guess' when we read, and sometimes incorrectly. [Show Figure 5.4 on the overhead projector for five seconds.] If you look carefully at the words on the left, you will see that 'the' has been written twice. In the words on the right, 'in' has been written twice. People often miss out the extra word because they are reading for meaning. They are guessing what should be there. We must not try to stop children guessing, but do try and encourage your child to guess sensibly. Do this by reading the sentence with the word missed out. You could ask: 'What word might fit in?'

Figure 5.4

Question: My child is a good reader, but he is not *interested* in books. What do I do?
Answer: The simple answer is that all children can be interested in books. The challenge
               is to find the right books and then to read them to the child.
Question: How much time do I need to spend on books?
Answer: This depends on the child. The answer is to make reading sessions regular. It is
               better to have 20 minutes each day than two hours once a week.
Question: I've done everything I can to get him to read, but we just end up quarrelling.
               What can I do?
Answer: Come in to school and let's see whether we can solve it together.

Drawing the threads together – the contract

To sum up, the speaker might say something like this:

'You've heard about the research and about the contribution you can make. The school is now committed to parental involvement in promoting children's reading.

    In essence you are asked to share a book with your child for 20 minutes a day. You are asked to make a daily comment on your child's reading and to ensure that the booklet supplied comes back to school each day.

    You will have the opportunity to participate in twice-termly Caper workshop sessions and to attend a termly Caper reading clinic.

    For our part, we shall offer a wide range of children's literature, advice and guidance to parents who want to participate fully in the project and the prospect of significant gains in your child's reading abilities. Thank you all for coming.'

CHAPTER 6
Bright ideas in the classroom

First meeting with staff

If a school is introducing Caper, even to one class, it is vital that a full pre-scheme staff meeting is held. Everyone then has an insight into the scheme. It is suggested that this meeting could be addressed by the teachers who wish to introduce Caper to their classrooms.

At this meeting the contribution made by the class teachers to the project is outlined. The three main requests made of staff are that they share:

- a belief in the potential of the project or at least an open mind about it (it has been demonstrated that an optimistic view of the potential of the project is crucial to its success);
- a willingness to present the Caper scheme as 'fun' and as an exciting bonus for the children (it is *not* homework!);
- a readiness to adjust classroom routine to accommodate the Caper scheme and to maintain the home–school link, through the Comment Booklet.

One should refer to the sensitivities and anxieties that parents may have in the school setting and the differences between 'helping' and 'teaching'. It needs to be stressed that the extent of parent involvement is very much up to the school.

The Caper Daily Comment Booklet

This is the essential link between home and school. The children put their booklets in a tray in the Caper corner of the classroom as they come in each day.

The teacher reviews and initials Comment Booklets when convenient. This takes about 10–15 minutes each day. Some teachers may have reservations about this time allocation, but it is a small price to pay for gaining two hours per week extra language activity for each child at home. At the end of the school day the teacher returns the Booklets to the children, praising those who have had them filled in. Even when there was not time to read, parents should be encouraged to make a comment. 'Didn't read' or 'Had to go to the Supermarket' maintains the dialogue.

Every 3 weeks the teacher makes a short comment back to the parents in the space provided. If a 'critical' comment is made, it should be balanced by a positive statement, e.g. 'Your comments appear to have dried up ... and after such a good start.' One effective comment to parents is simply: 'I do so enjoy reading your comments.'

The importance of this Daily Comment Booklet cannot be over-stated. Your individual response to parents shows them that you have noticed and it maintains the schemes momentum.

One Caper mother, an ex-teacher, commented:

'I always thought that I was a good mum, reading aloud to my children and hearing them read regularly. I would have said I did so every day. It was only the Comment Booklet that showed me how often I had missed.'

It is often the children who pressurise the parents into listening, once the project is established. If this starts to happen, it is a sure sign that you are generating real enthusiasm among the children in your class.

To protect the Comment Booklets, wallets can be issued to the children to carry the booklets between home and school. These can be:

- *plastic wallets*, from any major educational supplies company; these are fairly durable and waterproof and have the added advantage of conferring status on those children who are participating in the project;
- *class-made wallets*, using folded stapled card; these have the merit of being self-designed and the class can illustrate them with some thematic drawings, e.g. bonfires, Christmas, pets, seasons or faces; they need renewing every half-term and thus provide fresh impetus for the project; most Caper teachers have favoured them.

Guidance bookmarks

Many parents are not aware of their children's reading ability and cannot judge the difficulty level of books; this quickly becomes apparent in their daily comments. These problems are met by the teacher placing one of three 'guidance to parents bookmarks' into the Caper books each time they are changed (Figure 6.1). These are made by the class teacher on card and laminated. The bookmarks are particularly useful in the early weeks of the project with children whose parents have not heard them read for some time. After a while they become less important as parents tune in to their children's reading. Do not write page numbers on the bookmarks. Caper is not a race or a competition.

Maintaining children's enthusiasm

If the Caper is presented as something routine and mundane, then it will quickly lose momentum. For many children, the project provides the first chance that they will have to read a whole 'real' book themselves. Hence the teacher must attempt to maximise the project's impact on the class.

The following suggestions will help to sustain pupils' enthusiasm and interest.

CAPER

Talk about the picture.

Let your child read the story.

Give plenty of praise.

CAPER

Talk about the picture.

Share the reading.

If stuck, say the word.

CAPER

Talk about the picture.

Read the story to your child.

Please keep commenting.

Figure 6.1 Guidance bookmarks

Individual activities

- Allow the children to change books as they return them, but present such an opportunity as a reward or a treat. Changing Caper books should be an event for the child.
- At an appropriate time, invite the children to report on their Caper book – not on its level of difficulty, but on the content of the story. As 'favourite books' emerge, devise a waiting list, to be mounted on the wall, to prevent any squabbling over whose turn comes next. Large queues will quickly form for books that children have found to be a good read.
- Prepare giant picture cloze activities from selected texts to use to introduce children to new books (Figures 6.2–6.4). Either children can draw an appropriate picture in each space, or the teacher can prepare a selection of illustrations. These give the children a chance to sample a text in a light-hearted manner before committing themselves to taking the book home. The exercise teaches children another means of finding out about a book before making a choice.
- Review sheets are an excellent way of encouraging critical engagement and a creative response from children to what they have read. They emphasise to children and parents that reading requires an imaginative or critical response. Examples of review sheets will be found in Figures 6.5–6.8.

Mrs Wobble the Waitress

_____ was a waitress. When she carried a _____, it wobbled. She wobbled a bowl of _____. The soup landed on a customer's _____. It barked. Then she wobbled with a roast _____. The chicken landed on a customer's best _____. Her hat was ruined. The _____ sacked poor Mrs Wobble. She went home to her _____ who tried to cheer her up.

Figure 6.2 Example of a giant picture cloze: Mrs Wobble the waitress

The ENORMOUS crocodile

The enormous crocodile crept over to a place where there were a lot of coconut trees. He knew that children from the town often came here looking for ☐ .

There were always some coconuts on the ground that had fallen down.

The enormous crocodile quickly collected all the coconuts that were lying on the ground. He also gathered together several fallen ☐ .

"Now for Clever Trick Number One!" he whispered to himself. "It won't be long before I am eating the first part of my ☐ !"

Figure 6.3 Example of a giant picture cloze: the enormous crocodile

'Mister Magnolia' by Quentin Blake

Mr Magnolia has only one ☐ . He has an old ☐ that goes rooty-tooty, and two lovely sisters who play on the ☐ , but Mr Magnolia has only one ☐ . In his pond, live a ☐ , and a ☐ and a ☐ . He has green ☐ who pick holes in his suit, and some very fat ☐ who are learning to hoot. He gives rides to his friends when he goes for a ☐ .

Figure 6.4 Example of a giant picture cloze: Mr Magnolia

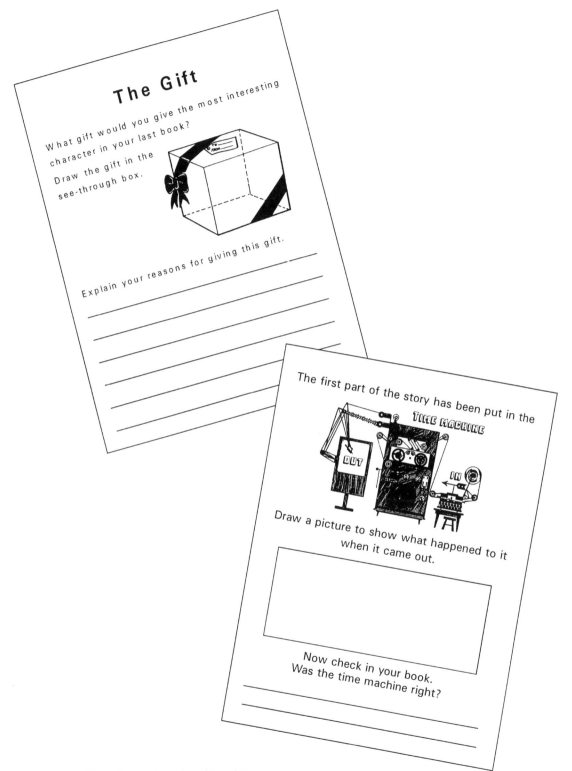

Figure 6.5 Examples of review sheets

Figure 6.6   More examples of review sheets

Figure 6.7 Example of another review sheet

Figure 6.8   Example of a further review sheet

Group activities

The following ideas will help to maintain the momentum of the project:

- A daily review. Teachers find that using the first 15 minutes of class time to discuss the previous night's reading with the children forms a positive focal point. Such discussion is an ideal opportunity to introduce the technical vocabulary of reading (author, title, illustrator and so on) even with the very youngest children in the scheme.
- Choosing a book. The teacher reads extracts from three or four books and asks the children which of the books they would most like to read and why. This helps children to understand that books are best chosen for their text, and not for their covers.
- Theme readings. The teacher introduces the idea of a theme to the class; this may mean anything from concrete concepts, such as books about monsters, to more abstract themes, e.g. 'being lonely' stories. This is a very successful activity that gives recognition to the experience of books that the children have gained with their parents.
- Drama activities. Items from a book that is particularly popular with the class can form the focus for a mime or even a scripted piece of dialogue. (Try *Not Now Bernard* by David McKee as a mime!)
- Percussive retelling. Take a story, e.g. *Three Billy Goats Gruff*; by using clappers for goats one, two and three, a drum for the troll and a cacophony for the final splash, the narration can be effectively highlighted. This is a technique familiar to early years. Many other texts lend themselves to this approach.
- A shared review. A group of four children is given the opportunity to read a book and then to present the group's views on it to the class as a whole.

The mathematics curriculum

It is important to keep a record of a child's reading development and experience. Children are always being asked how their reading is coming along and it is an essential part of the teacher's role to provide them with the verbal routines, the vocabulary and the recording activities which allow them to do this.

- A straw poll. Conduct a 'straw poll' of favourite books, authors or types of book. Young children quickly learn to discuss books as true stories, animal tales, fantasies and so on. This can form part of the essential introduction that children need to different types of text or genre. It helps with reading by enabling the reader to predict more accurately what kind of language and what vocabulary lie ahead.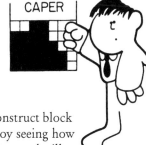
- Block graphs. Use the information from the straw poll to construct block graphs for display on the classroom wall. The children enjoy seeing how their preferences change over time and at the same time the graphs illus-

trate the children's expanding knowledge of books. It is interesting to note which old favourites remain popular throughout.

- Line graphs. As an example, note the number of Caper booklets returned during the fourth week of every term 'to see how well we are doing as a class'.
- A ratings chart. Make a card index of all the books in the lending stock; then, as the children finish a book, they find the title in the card index and put their rating, from 1 to 5, of the book on the card: 1 = boring; 5 = excellent (Figure 6.11). This helps children to check whether their friends rate the book a 'good read'.

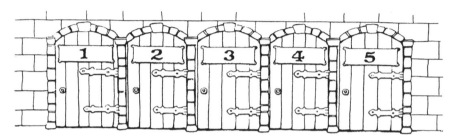

Competitions

Many ideas are used by the Caper teachers to mount in-class book competitions, but the following competition is based on a quiz that a Caper teacher set to maintain the momentum of the scheme during the holiday (Figure 6.9). The school offered three book prizes to the winners.

If you decide to set a quiz of your own, consult the local branch library first as to the availability of the books concerned.

Display

Caper teachers have used the following display ideas to add excitement to their classrooms:

- *life-size favourite characters* (which are easily drawn by making acetate copies of the illustrations in books and then enlarging them using the overhead projector;
- *frieze*, taken from the class 'book of the month';
- *comic strips*;
- *murals*, e.g. from a scene in *Where the Wild Things Are* by Maurice Sendak (Bodley Head; Picture Puffin);
- *character quiz* asking which books characters come from (using illustrations and quotations from key figures in some favourite books);
- *collage* of a popular book to which every member of the class can make some contribution;

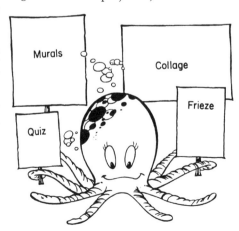

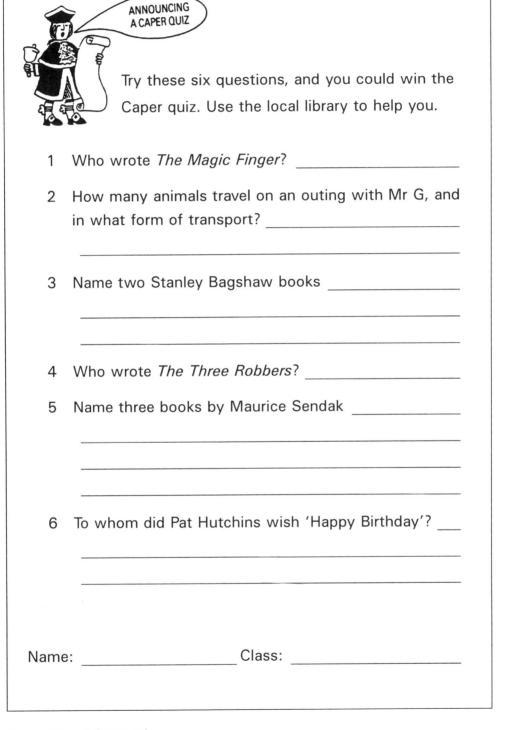

Figure 6.9   A Caper quiz

- *posters* for the film of the book ('now showing', 'final week', 'award winner' and so on);
- *giant scrapbooks* of favourite stories;
- *zigzag* books.

CHAPTER 7
Caper reading clinics

Having asked parents to read with their children on a daily basis, we were shocked by the difficulty that this task was presenting to some parents. Reading together created family tensions and friction and could be a negative experience for both children and parents. Many parents made excessive demands upon young children's reading and became frustrated when their children failed to meet their expectations. There was often a battle over reading, leading parents to abandon what seemed an uphill task.

A short session of practical individual guidance made all the difference.

Parents are invited to an individual clinic once a term. These sessions last, on average, 20 minutes. They provide an opportunity for parents:

- to demonstrate their listening skills;
- to raise any questions about their children's reading;
- to broaden their listening skills.

The critical target is encouraging parents to be positive interactive listeners who understand their children's efforts at reading.

More than 80% of parents attended the clinics in the initial Caper schools; in some schools this figure was nearer 100%. In research undertaken to evaluate the Caper project with 3–4-year-olds it appeared that it was always the more enthusiastic schools (and within those the more enthusiastic teachers) that had the highest strike rates. Schools where morale was high and who expected good levels of parental participation generally had the result that they were aiming for.

Some parents need several invitations and considerable notice in order to be able to attend. The class teacher should send out the invitations four days before the clinic is to be held; then, if anyone cannot make a particular time, further invitations can be made so that there is a full list of parents to be seen. One way of dealing with this is to see one parent with his or her child at the close of afternoon school each day. In this way the parents of an entire class can be seen in one half-term. Evaluation in the early years demonstrated that parents unable to make the first meeting were just as committed to their children's education as those who *were* able to attend.

What goes on in the clinic session?

If parents do not respond to the first invitation to clinic sessions, then it is important to review the style of the school's approach; for example, parents may see the offer of help as too threatening, despite our efforts to the contrary. It may help to ask those who attend what they think about the invitation.

Parents meet their children at the classroom prior to the clinic session. Each child has a favourite Caper book and a Comment Booklet to use in the session. For every appointment, the organisers should make sure that they have the name of the child and the *parent* beforehand. The parent's and the child's surname may not be the same; be aware of any sensitive areas ahead of time.

This is an opportunity to observe the child and the parent reading together. Reading is being portrayed as a shared experience; so the parent, child and teacher sit together alongside a table and *not* across the table from each other. Note how they sit together, and whether they are at ease. Some parents may need reassurance to put them at their ease to recreate home reading.

Ask how they have been reading together. What have they enjoyed? What difficulties have they encountered?

Explain that your aim in this session is to observe them listening together and to see how you can be of help.

At this point ask the parent and the child to show you how they read at home together. Watch their interaction. Do they seem comfortable sharing the book? During the session the emphasis is upon the parent's listening performance and *not* upon the child's reading skills. The focus then is how the parent is supporting reading.

The use of a familiar 'easy' text reassures the child and results in a more representative reading performance. The child is then asked to choose a book from a selection of slightly harder material. The choice of book is left to the child. This provides an opportunity to chat about reasons for choosing any one book. It may take three or four books to gain an adequate impression of a parent's listening skills.

Caution is necessary when giving advice, as reading is a topic on which parents often hold firm views. They may have uncertain recall of their own reading development. For some, learning to read may have been very challenging and some may have had an unsympathetic teacher. On the other hand, people do not always remember their difficulties in becoming literate. They may compress their own steady progress in reading into a sudden leap into fluency and find it difficult to sympathise with their children and the problems they face. One can remember not being able to ride a bicycle and then being able to. We are looking at the area between these two states.

In asking parents to broaden their listening repertoire, the organiser should be prepared to *demonstrate* any technique that she or he discusses with them. It is so valuable for parents to be given a good model.

The advice is in the form of small changes in listening techniques. No one should be overloaded with help; one or two suggestions are the limit for any one session.

These termly one-to-one consultations aim for *gradual* development of good listening techniques.

The organiser should advise parents:

- that any new technique should be practised inter-mittently and not used during every listening session;
- that it would help if any difficulties in trying out new techniques were noted in the daily comment booklet.

The teacher notes any advice offered to a parent during a clinic session and is thus well prepared for that parent's subsequent visits to school.

The list of topics dealt with in clinic sessions is substantial and only a limited number of the subjects raised by parents is covered here. The advice offered is simply an outline response as each teacher will bring his or her own knowledge to bear upon situations as they arise. The suggestions in this section will be helpful in responding to parents' queries about how they should help, whether or not it is decided to organise structured 'clinics'. The advice given has also been used in training non-teaching assistants and volunteers within school.

Setting the right climate in the clinic session

The aim of the clinic session is to emphasise the school's view that reading together has to be a fun activity. It is not a dour experience in learning. Parents want to know how well their children are coming along with their reading, and there are plenty of opportunities for school to keep parents informed. The clinic session is there to demonstrate the school's commitment to reading as a quality experience rather than simply as a progressive movement through a reading scheme.

The purpose of the clinic is not to assess children's reading, or to examine parents as listeners, but rather to advise how parents might best support their children's reading. The teacher's role is advisory, and not prescriptive.

In talking about books, in handling books and in listening to children read from books, the teacher must demonstrate his or her own enthusiasm for children's fiction and his or her awareness of the magic to be found in a good story. The teacher must present a good role model for parents, throughout each session.

CHAPTER 8
How to listen to children read

In the Caper clinics for parents, a wide range of issues on hearing children read comes up. This section gives suggested answers which may be raised. Teachers should read this section before the clinic session.

When is the best time?

Many parents are apt to listen to their children read at bedtime. Others set a definite time, e.g. six o'clock. Parents have commented that bedtime might be not be the best time for young children to read. Bedtime is often portrayed as an idyllic 'quiet time', whereas in reality it is a very busy part of the day. Children may quickly latch on to a ritual of bedtime reading that a parent cannot sustain.

The advice offered to parents has been to try to listen to their children at the same point during the evening, e.g. just after tea, rather than listening to them read last thing at night. Some early risers find 20 minutes for reading before or after breakfast.

Observation

Observing a child read, i.e. actually looking at him or her rather than at the text, is an important listening skill. Watching a child's eye, head and hand movement will indicate the strategies being employed by the young reader faced with an unfamiliar word, e.g. looking at the picture, reading back, reading forward, beginning to sound out the unknown word and finally looking up at the helper. The enabling helper should supply the unknown word just after the child begins to sound out the unknown word. Parents will need help to judge the best moment. Therefore, reading with a child requires listening and looking.

How much must we read?

'Little and often' covers this point. Caper advocates that parents should listen to their children read for not more than 20 minutes every night.

Parents are asked to end a listening session before their children's concentration starts to wander, or at least to take over the reading themselves. It is important to stress that all sessions should end at a meaningful point in the story, e.g. the end of a chapter or an incident, and *not* in mid-sentence or at the bottom of page. Stopping at a high interest point sustains enthusiasm, as all soap opera fans will confirm.

Praise; how can I?

Many parents report initial problems in setting the right tone for the reading sessions at home. Prior to receiving guidance from school that reading together should be fun some parents may have been over critical in their approach and corrected children too much. They sometimes speak of their own children's surprise when parents become supportive rather than critical listeners.

Any problems disappear as their children become used to parents' new-found pleasure in their efforts at reading. If parents continue to over correct, teacher may have to negotiate between a child and a parent as to the most appropriate method of sharing a book together. A child may consider a particular phrase used by her mother as being childish and inappropriate now that she is in Year 2!

This may seem trivial, but such hiccups can prove a real obstacle to effective listening and to a parent and a child getting maximum pleasure from their sessions together.

Parents generally give insufficient praise, but praise which is not sincere will quickly be seen as such. The teacher should emphasise how well, in fact, a child is reading, by pointing to those skills which are being exercised and are passing unnoticed. It is not just the amount of praise that has to be right; praise has to be perceived by a child as earned.

Talking about pictures

Many parents find it difficult to talk about the story when they share a book with their children. If so, the teacher must demonstrate how discussion of the picture leads children to saying many of the words in the adjacent text. All parents are encouraged to use this approach but the 'picture–chat' approach is most relevant to children who are struggling with a text that they find demanding. If the organiser is confident that a child already utilises all the clues provided by the picture, then this advice may be superfluous, as the purpose of a good illustration is to encourage the flow of the story. It is *not* an opportunity to engage a child in some 'teaching' diversion,

e.g. 'How *many* trees?' or 'What colour is the dog?' Some parents will need reminding that reading together is not supposed to be a 'teaching exercise'.

Favourite and easy books

Caper is attempting to develop a connection in children's minds between reading and pleasure. For this reason, plenty of easy-to-read books should be available. A book that is a 'good' book and easy to read is likely to be enjoyed. Many children in Caper will, given a free choice, always select a very simple text, sometimes revisiting the same book more than once. Parents need to be reassured that children enjoy repeating successful experiences and that the re-reading of a favourite text is worthwhile and not unusual. Parents should consider such favourites as possible presents.

It may be that the child is playing safe with reading and is not yet ready to take risks with more complex texts while his or her parent is listening. The clinic is an opportunity to demonstrate to the parent how to give extra support when young readers tackle more challenging material.

Guessing

Their children's tendency to guess at unfamiliar words in new contexts causes some parents anxiety. They need to be reminded that guessing or predicting is *an absolute essential*. It is important to enquire in detail about the nature of this 'guessing' and the manner in which the parent has responded to it in the past.

- If the guessing is completely wild and the word offered bears no relation to either the sense of the story, or the initial letter sounds of the word in the text, then the parent may be leaving the child 'stuck' for too long. As a result, the child offers a word to fill the void rather than wait in silence for the listener's help. The solution is for the parent to give the correct word sooner.
- If the guesses tend to correspond to the initial sounds of the given word in the text, then the parent praises the child for his or her effort and asks for a word that makes sense. 'Good, you've begun with the right sound; can you think of a word that begins with that sound and makes sense in the story?' This may seem a little cumbersome and should only be tried occasionally, but it does reinforce the value of guessing.
- If the child's guessing tends to make *sense* within the context of the story but bears little relation to the phonic structure of the word in the text, then parents must be cautioned against inhibiting such guessing. The child's attention can be drawn to the initial letter sound in the word and asked to guess for sense again, but the parent should beware of interrupting the flow of the story unduly.
- Without this skill of 'guessing for sense', the young reader would be ill equipped to tackle an unknown text without adult listening support. Indeed rather than inhibit the flow of the story, the listener should accept the substituted word, provided that the integrity of the story is maintained. The listener may wish to return to the 'guessed word' at the end of the tale. However, such reviewing needs to be handled with sensitivity, e.g. 'That was a good guess, it made sense; the word was ———.' Review initiated by the child (self-correction) is, of course, encouraged.

It may be necessary to demonstrate to the parent through a cloze activity (see the workshop session on p. 67) that guessing is an essential element in reading. Discouraging a child from guessing at print will inhibit the development of fluent reading. The child who has not learnt to guess without anxiety is generally reduced to inappropriate 'voice pointing' or painful 'sounding out'.

Pointing and voice pointing

Many parents continue to point at words or encourage their children to do so, long after it serves as a positive aid to reading. If this is the case, try to demonstrate to the parent:

- that the child can read without pointing;
- that the pointing hand or ruler may be obscuring other information in the text that the child needs to generate the word that he or she is stuck on.

Many children who read well regress to pointing if they begin to read more complex texts or books with a smaller print size than they are used to. Their style of reading changes dramatically with changes in the nature of the text. Compare a child's reading of straightforward narrative with allusive or figurative texts (e.g. poetry), or with instructive material. A child's reading style can be more or less mature depending on what they are reading. Style cannot be judged from the approach to one text alone.

The problem of voice pointing is common. It stems from attempts to decode a word correctly as a simple isolated entity, separated from its context. This may be the result of reading by pointing, where the child's concept of reading is to voice in isolation the word indicated by the pointing finger. It may help if the teacher models the sentence that the child has just read and then asks the child to say it again in a 'talking voice'. Children can read with expression through example and with familiar texts. This process can be augmented by the parent using praise for phrasing and expression.

'Stuck' strategies

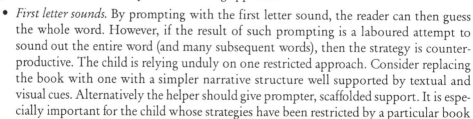

In the initial talk to parents, the emphasis is placed upon the parent's saying the word that the child is stuck on and in giving the word earlier rather than later. Children tell you soon enough if you are providing the word too quickly, whereas they tend to struggle in silence if there is a delay. Once the listening partnership is established, further suggestions may be made to broaden the parents' listening approach.

- *First letter sounds.* By prompting with the first letter sound, the reader can then guess the whole word. However, if the result of such prompting is a laboured attempt to sound out the entire word (and many subsequent words), then the strategy is counterproductive. The child is relying unduly on one restricted approach. Consider replacing the book with one with a simpler narrative structure well supported by textual and visual cues. Alternatively the helper should give prompter, scaffolded support. It is especially important for the child whose strategies have been restricted by a particular book to be reminded in this way that different strategies are essential. The strategies that a child uses are as much determined by the book as by anything else. A simpler text allows the child to practise being a reader again.

- *Read up to.* Where appropriate, the listener can suggest that the child re-reads up to the 'stuck' word. Often this gives the necessary cue to the reader, who carries on without undue interruption. Again, the purpose of this activity is to help the child to develop appropriate reading strategies. It is done once or perhaps twice in a session. More than this and the flow of the story is broken.
- *Read on and guess back.* Similarly, the child can be encouraged to leave out the word that he or she is stuck on, read on to the end of the sentence and guess back at the unknown word. By placing the missing word into a meaningful context, the reader may be able to guess the unknown word using syntactic and semantic clues in the text. Many children develop these strategies for themselves. Others need to be shown that this is a good way to discover the unknown word.
- *Clueing.* The listener can be shown how to 'clue' the child into the unknown word. For example, if the text reads: 'The horses had not eaten any food for five days and they were *starving*', where 'starving' is the unknown word, then the question, 'How would you feel if you hadn't eaten for five days?' might produce an acceptable guess. Providing clues in this manner encourages reading for meaning and the development of a child's repertoire of reading strategies. Use this technique when the missing word lends itself to such an approach.

Exchanging roles

The clinics tell us how parents perceive reading and how they read with their children. One mother demonstrated how, once the 20 minutes was up, she might occasionally re-read a paragraph that had caused confusion and ask her son to spot any mistakes that she had made. Mother and son readily demonstrated this technique and the boy visibly relished the role of editor for his mother's reading. While this activity produces an unusual stress on reading for precision, not necessarily in the spirit of Caper, the fun element was very evident. Mother and child had evolved an effective habit of reading together for pleasure, and this is the key to successful collaboration. Advice and guidance should always be balanced against the dangers of disrupting an effective parent–child interaction.

CHAPTER 9
Other ways of listening

In the clinic sessions and through feedback from the Daily Comment Booklet a small proportion of parents are evidently in need of further help. There will be some who get very stuck. Their children are struggling and they are too. There is the parent who is striving too hard and who believes in a simple link between effort and progress. Sometimes a parent may have had problems learning themselves, and supporting their child's reading may be bringing back unhappy memories. Parents whose children have significant reading delay often need extra guidance. Patience can wear thin if you seem to be making little progress. Teachers have to make a judgement on who may need advice on special techniques or approaches for fostering reading.

Further guidance may need to be offered to three broad groups of parents.

- The first group consists of those who find it difficult to listen to their children read because of doubts about their *own* literacy. Experience with such parents has been that overwhelmingly they underestimate their reading ability but, where these doubts are well founded, then the parent may need to recruit another listener or may adopt a more passive listening role. In such an instance the school's interest may trigger the parent to seek help from an adult basic skills group. It is suggested that the teacher tactfully explores the coping strategies which these parents use to deal with the literacy demands of everyday life. It is important not to over-react to an admission of illiteracy, as the parents may feel that they have divulged a secret which they should have kept. Remember that the standard of an effective helper's reading does not have to be extraordinarily high. Once you can show such a parent *how* he or she can help, you will have two people at least in the family with a keen interest in the scheme, both of whose reading can grow together.

- The second group consists of those parents who find it difficult to hear their children read because of the children's behaviour or learning problems. These problems, whether real or imagined, require a positive response from the school. The focus will be upon ensuring success with books well within the children's compass, of rewarding success and engaging the pupil fully in planning the reading programme. Developing reading skills has the potential to improve behaviour significantly.

- The third group consists of those parents who have failed to involve themselves in the scheme or have children whose reading is not progressing. The very few intractable problems of this kind which arise will need more intensive help. Regular reviewing of the comment booklet will highlight who these parents are. Additional advice and support may also be available through your school's special educational needs coordinator.

The techniques described so far have been found to assist parents in promoting their children's reading. Other more specialised techniques with which teachers should be familiar include paired reading and shadowed or simultaneous reading.

Paired and shadowed reading

Bushell *et al.* (1982) and Morgan and Lyon (1979) reported these techniques in detail. Paired reading is most familiarly associated with the work of Keith Topping (1995).

In the authors' experience, both of these can be tricky and definitely need to be modelled. Unless one is crystal clear about how they work, parents will become very confused; hence it is essential to practise them first, before introducing the techniques to parents.

Simultaneous or shadowed reading

This is called 'simultaneous reading' in the literature; however, the word 'shadowing' describes the technique more accurately. In its simplest form, a child and an adult begin to read aloud together. The parent is asked to read slightly behind the child so that the child attacks the first sound of every word. The child attempts every word. The parent simply completes the word that the child gets stuck on, allowing the child to self-correct if a mistake has been made. If in the sentence given, the child could not read the word 'engine', then what effectively happens is as follows:

Child:	'T	he	b	lue	t	rain	s	tood	b	ehind	t	he	e	. . . ngine.'
Parent:		'The		blue		train		stood		behind		the		engine.'

The parent begins to read every word one sound behind the child. However, as the parent is reading naturally, with no undue stress upon the difficult words, he or she often completes the word at the same time as the child. The value of this is clearly shown when the child cannot say a word. The child begins the word by saying the first sound and the parent's correct (but not correcting) prompt enables him or her to 'read' the unknown word while maintaining the flow of the story. The value of the technique is that it can be used to help the parent to adjust to the child's own pace when reading aloud. At the same time, the parent learns not to stress any particular word, so that the child never gains the impression that he or she is about to attempt the reading equivalent of Beecher's Brook.

Difficulties which may need to be dealt with in the approach, are as follows:

- Parents may be reading too quickly, outpacing the child.
- Parents can become stuck on this particular strategy to the exclusion of others.
- This strategy can give over-emphasis to words that the child cannot decode.
- Context guessing is minimised in this approach.

Advantages of the approach are:

- the ease with which books are read;
- the consequent reduction in pressure on the child.

It is necessary to stress the need to 'take time out' from the strategy to ensure that the child is understanding what has been read, for instance by talking about the story or its characters.

Once the teacher is confident that this approach is working well for both the child and the parent (usually this takes about two to four weeks), then consideration might be given to moving the partnership on to paired reading.

Paired reading

This is a very well-known and researched technique. There is still debate about its effectiveness, with some studies reporting huge gains in terms of rapid progress on reading tests. The technique taught to the parents is deceptively simple:

- The parent and the child begin to read together as in shadowed reading.
- When the child wishes to read on his or her own, he or she squeezes or taps the listener's hand.
- This signal 'knocks out' or 'shuts up' the listener.
- As soon as the child reads even one word correctly, the listener praises him or her.
- The child continues to read alone until he or she gets stuck or makes a mistake.
- The listener says the correct word, and allows the child to repeat it. This support must be prompt, within one second, or the child is left embarrassed and uncomfortable, waiting for the unknown word. Then both begin to read together again as in shadowing.
- As soon as the child wants to read on his or her own, he or she squeezes the listener's hand or knocks again and takes over.

The principal advantage of paired reading is that it enables a child to take control of the reading interaction. This turns the traditional approach on its head and is immediately very attractive to young readers. In this approach the parent is seen very much as a resource.

It takes at least 20 minutes to coach parents in this listening technique. It requires patience to apply and greater input from parents. Parents have to listen actively.

The progress of the partnership is monitored at intervals of two–three weeks and, when the technique seems to be operating properly, the parent is encouraged to allow mistakes to see whether the child can self-correct from the context of the story.

Although paired reading is arguably expensive in terms of the time needed to train and sustain individual parents, once the technique has been mastered it has been shown to work well. Paired reading:

- maximises the child's independent reading;
- removes any sense of failure;
- allows the child to attempt to read anything;
- involves the child as a 'partner' in the reading process.

Experience has shown that it is difficult for parents to sustain their use of this technique. Negotiating a realistic time limit of say 10–12 weeks helps to keep parents on target, as does the fortnightly monitoring. After 12 weeks, if the parent and child wish to continue with this approach, they can do so, while those who are finding it hard going can revert to less demanding approaches without losing face. The checklist in Figure 9.1 can be sent home periodically to monitor progress in paired reading.

Finally, a few parents may use the clinic session to introduce wider topics, perhaps personal problems. If this happens, the teacher can either provide a supportive listening ear or suggest other avenues of support within the community which could be accessed through the school nurse, the family doctor, or the school psychologist.

PARENTS' CHECKLIST

Are you and your child reading together?

Daily _____ Every other day _____ Twice a week_____

Are you adjusting your listening to enable your child to enjoy the book?

Yes/No

Are you adjusting to the pace of your child?   Yes/No

Does your child try to read every word?   Yes/No

Does your child remember to knock or squeeze?

Always_____ Sometimes _____ Never _____

Do you respond to your child's knock or squeeze?   Yes/No

Do you manage to praise promptly when he or she knocks to take charge of the reading?   Yes/No

Are you managing to ignore minor errors?   Yes/No

Does reading together begin again smoothly when he or she gets stuck?   Yes/No

Are you using the paired reading approach?

Always_____ Sometimes _____ Rarely _____

Are there any aspects of your reading together that are causing concern?

_____

_____

_____

_____

Signed : _____ **Listener to:** _____ **Date:** _____

Figure 9.1   Suggested parents' checklist if children are using the paired reading approach

CHAPTER 10
Parent workshops

The primary function of the parent workshops is to help parents to help their children to develop fluent literacy skills, but the workshops aim to achieve more than this. They are designed to bring parents up to date with the new thinking in schools about literacy teaching. Parents' questions about the Literacy Strategy can be answered and schools can respond to the reservations which parents may express. Workshops signify the regard that school has for the essential parent role and give a stamp of approval to the school–parent partnership. The workshops on genre and on poetry give parents further insight into Literacy Hour activities and extend the work that parents and children can do together to support literacy development.

The National Literacy Strategy – Framework for Teaching (Department for Education and Employment 1998b) specifies a term-by-term focus for children's reading and writing. The workshops, which are intended to be delivered on a half-termly basis, reflect this structure. The workshops help to extend parents' understanding of literacy teaching in school as children progress through the programme objectives each term. In introducing parents to the strategy structure, the workshops provide a further bridge between home and school and give a very helpful impetus to the child–parent dialogue.

If the workshops are to be held during the school day, many parents will bring younger children with them. To enhance the sense of welcome, have some toys available for these children. The presence of very young children gives the workshop organiser the opportunity to raise the point that some youngsters, when reading aloud, cannot tolerate distractions. The workshop organiser can comment upon how hard it must be with brothers and sisters around to give 20 minutes a day to just one child at a time. Parents generally enjoy this recognition of their efforts to help with children's reading within a busy family context.

Each workshop consists of three activities, including a suggested home activity and, where applicable, a review of that activity.

Workshops include an activity similar to those that children work on during the Literacy Hour, an activity designed to extend understanding of the reading process and introduce a number of key literacy terms.

Many parents use the workshop setting as an opportunity to raise questions about children's reading and problems which their children may be experiencing. These will need to be explored while maintaining the integrity of the workshop session. The discovery that similar problems have been encountered by others helps to reduce anxiety and puts their own child's performance into perspective. Parents derive comfort and reassurance from sharing their difficulties with a supportive group.

Everyone should be encouraged to contribute and have their views listened to. Just as in classroom teaching the leader must ensure that everyone in the room has the opportunity to contribute and that no one group or individual dominates proceedings. If a question cannot be answered immediately, the organiser should offer to bring a reply to the next workshop session. Experience shows that parents welcome such candour and it is a strong element in maintaining rapport. Be on the look out for useful advice from the group for school. This should always be noted and discussed with the head teacher. Evidence that you have acted upon positive advice carries a powerful message about your view of the group.

Workshops should not last for more than an hour. A brisk pace needs to be sustained just as during the Literacy Hour.

Five games are described at the end of this chapter. They can be used as fun activities at the beginning of a workshop, which will help to break the ice.

The most successful workshops are held in a classroom or library setting. Sometimes only a hall is available for use, but a group of 30 parents, in a hall built for 200, can feel insecure and uncomfortable. Tea and biscuits provided for those attending enhances their sense of welcome to school.

Whenever possible a member of staff from another class attends the workshop. This lightens the load and helps to generate a school rather than a class approach to reading and to delivering workshops. A big plus for having another member of staff attend is that it ensures that the workshop does not spill over into a complaints session about the functioning of the school or the performance of any one teacher. Having a second teacher present may also gain another convert to the potential of parental involvement in reading!

For some workshop activities you will need to produce an overhead transparency (OHT) from an original in the text. These can easily be created using the school photocopier, but do make sure that they are the kind that will withstand the temperature generated in the photocopying process. 'Niceday' OHP Transparency Film works well. If preferred, the originals can be photocopied on plain paper and distributed to each parent.

Outline workshop calendar

The outline workshop calendar is as follows:

Workshop	Date
1	3 weeks after the starts
2	2 weeks after half-term
3	2 weeks after the beginning of the spring term
4	2 weeks after the spring half-term
5	2 weeks after the beginning of the summer term

Workshop I: How children make sense of text

This workshop includes text level and word level activities. The purpose is:

- to review how the scheme is progressing;
- to explore in a preliminary way ideas about books;
- to explore ideas about reading;
- to look at how children learn letters.

The resources necessary are:

- a Caper Book for each parent;
- paper and pencils for Activity 4;
- OHTs 1, 2 and 3 for workshop 1 (alternatively have photocopies of each OHT for every parent);
- overhead projector.

Activity 1: Review of the project so far

This is the first workshop in the year and follows the initial parent meeting. You will need, therefore, to review the progress of the scheme so far this term. The content of Activity 1 is largely generated by the parents themselves. Questions are raised concerning the routine functioning of the project and the leader is able to offer guidance where there is any uncertainty. Many parents will report that their children are eager to read aloud. The reasons for this will include:

- that there is no pressure, i.e. children are readily told the word when they get stuck;
- that children are now reading aloud to good supportive adult listeners;
- that children are being alerted to the fun to be had in good books.

Activity 2: Exploring views about the books that children are reading – text level activity

Give each parent a book from the Caper book stock and allow everyone five minutes to examine it.

A discussion explores these questions:

1. Would this book be of interest to your child?
2. Could your child read this book independently?
3. Could your child read this book with you supplying the word that he or she gets stuck on?

A diversity of views will arise on the difficulty and interest level of the books and parents' opinion of their children's reading ability. Draw together the threads of the discussion, emphasising that many children's books are written with interest ages of five, six, seven and eight but a reading age of 12 years plus. (Are these books necessarily excluded?) Then read some selected extracts to the parents to illustrate the dilemma, using, for example:

The Shrinking of Treehorn by Florence Parry Heide (Puffin Books);
The Day the Smells Went Wrong by Catherine Sefton (Puffin Books);
The Twits by Roald Dahl (Cape; Puffin Books);
How the Whale Became by Ted Hughes (Puffin Books);
The Wind in the Willows by Kenneth Grahame (Methuen).

First day at school

The _____ that my eldest _____ started at the _____ school was one of the _____ days of _____ life. She seemed excited _____ the way _____ the school but, once _____ the playground, she went _____ quiet.

The _____ rang; so I _____ her to her _____ teacher. As soon as _____ let _____ of her, _____ she burst _____ tears. I felt terrible; the _____ wanted _____ to _____ but I couldn't leave _____ like _____ .

Figure 10.1 Cloze exercise (Workshop 1, OHT 1)

Insight into reading

We guess at print

It is acceptable for children to guess.

We needed several attempts to get the word

Our children may need a little time to grasp the unknown word.

We leave out unknown words and guess back at them.

Children may need to be shown that this is acceptable when reading.

We change our guesses in the light of further reading.

If children guess we need to encourage them to refine their guessing or sense.

For *us* the 'right word' is the one that makes sense.

If our children make sense of the text, but make an occasional error, we should not make them sacrifice the flow of the story for precision.

Figure 10.2 Workshop 1, OHT 2

The point is made again that these stories interest the children, but some children may only gain access to them with the help of an interested adult. The key message is to give your child enough help to enjoy the book. In some instances this will mean that the parent does all the reading!

Activity 3: An introduction to reading strategies – text level activity

The cloze exercise (Figure 10.1) is used. Invite the parents as a group to fill in the spaces as you point to the words. Be sure to introduce the activity as a cloze exercise which is at the text level, thus keeping to Literacy Hour terminology. This particular text was written by a parent.

A range of lessons can be drawn from the passage; everyone will be familiar with the experience of their child's first day at school (and there will always be parents for whom this is the 'best' day of their lives!) and the point can be made that experienced narrative is always easier to work with. To begin with, efforts are hesitant but, as the territory and the task are recognised, confidence and strike rate increase. There will usually be one or two who get the idea and supply the words first. These are generally the parents who are themselves regular readers. Cloze exercises are such a useful way of building parents' appreciation of our approach in school to reading that they should feature often in home work and workshop activities. These exercises demonstrate that guessing is a crucial task and the exercise provides the opportunity for a discussion on its importance and meaning in a child's reading. The guesses that a child makes when reading will tell you how much or how little he or she is getting from the text; a child who is not guessing enough needs encouragement to take more risks and may need a little more adult support; the child who is guessing too much needs to be invited to pay more attention to the words on the page.

After discussing parents' responses to Figure 10.1, put up Figure 10.2. This summarises the insights that parents will have suggested during the discussion.

Activity 4: Learning letters – word level activity

Use Figure 10.3. Parents are issued with pencils and paper but asked not to write anything yet. The parents are asked to study the three groups of letters for about one minute; then the overhead projector is switched off and parents are asked to copy out what they remember.

Examine the parents' efforts at random and share their efforts with the group. Most parents recall the top line. This line may not necessarily be presented in order. Many parents space the letters equidistant from each other instead of grouping them in blocks of four.

Points to be drawn from the discussion are these:

1. Even in an apparently simple task such as this, adults will bring to bear experience and knowledge which children may not have. For example, because they know that text is read from left to right an adult's approach to the task is going to be more systematic than the child who may have no prior experience of a particular rule of written language. Beware of assuming that a task is easy for a child when it is not. This can all too easily lead to the annoyed parent and the tearful offspring.

```
rs   vt   bp
lm   ow   qd
```

Figure 10.3 Workshop 1, OHT 3 (after Clay 1979)

2. Even for the experienced reader, short-term memory is strictly limited, especially where what is to be remembered makes no sense. Few parents are able to recall more than eight letters; those who do will have unusually good memories or be employing a system to make sense of them. One parent memorised all 12 letters by making nonsense words out of them. This mnemonic technique formed the focus for further lively discussion.

In view of this it is not surprising:

- that children experience difficulties in making a phonic attack on long words;
- that they quickly forget words which they have already encountered in their reading.

Home activity

Each parent takes home a picture book from the classroom library and recreates the story with their child through the illustrations. The following work well:

I'm Going On A Dragon Hunt by Maurice Jones (Puffin Books);
Sunshine by Jan Ormerod (Puffin Books);
The Trunk by Brian Wildsmith (Oxford University Press);
Dogger by Shirley Hughes (Bodley Head; Armada Picture Lions).

Parents give sufficient help to enable the task to be completed without too much effort and as a collaborative enterprise. The parents may scribe the stories which their children tell. Each parent is given a couple of sheets of lined paper to write out the story. Completed stories are returned to the class teacher and form material for the opening activity of Workshop 2.

Workshop 2: Learning more about the reading process

This includes text level, sentence level and word level activities. The purposes are:

- to examine children's expressive skills;
- to look at how letters help us to guess words;
- to examine how the first letter and context helps with unknown words;
- to begin to look at story sequencing.

The resources required are:

- completed stories from Workshop 1, Home Activity;
- Workshop 2, OHT 1(Figure 10.4) OHT 2 (Figure 10.5) and OHT 3 (Figure 10.6);
- paper and pencils for Activity 2;
- story sequencing cards cut up and in envelopes;
- one set per parent for the home activity.

Activity 1 (home activity from previous workshop)

The workshop leader begins by thanking parents for their efforts, and notes that some of the stories were small books in themselves!

The points to stress are as follows:

- Children tell interesting exciting stories, using a considerable vocabulary. Illustrate these with readings from their stories.

Each dash represents a letter. Construct one word to fit the information given.

— — u — —

— — — — e — — — —

— — l — —

— — u — —

— — — d — — —

Figure 10.4   Workshop 2, OHT 1

Now try these words.

f — — — — — — — —

m — — — — — —

t — — —

l — — — —

p — — — — — — —

u — —

Figure 10.5   Workshop 2, OHT 2

- For the majority of young children there is a gulf between their expressive skills and their reading performance, the former being well in advance of the latter.
- Good adult listening support gives children access to stories that match their interests, thus maintaining their enthusiasm for books which they may not yet have the technical skills to read independently.

Activity 2: How letters help us guess words

Put up Figure 10.4, or alternatively make a photocopy for each participant. The task for the group is to guess a word with only one letter present. In Figure 10.4 the letter is in the middle of the word; for Figure 10.5 the first letter is given. The point of the exercise is to demonstrate how letters help in reading unknown words. The first letter of a word helps most.

Badger's speech

'Sad case,' murmured Doctor Mole, who seemed to know Fox well.

'Chemical burns. Factories, you know. We get plenty of those.'

'What do animals want with f — — — — — — — —?' Badger said.

He had been silent most of the m — — — — — — . 'Humans have nothing to teach us. We have gifts and skills that t — — — can never match. Besides we're quiet and orderly; we l — — — — no mess; we bring up our children p — — — — — — — . We don't eat humans; we don't use them as they u — — us, and we don't need their nasty inventions!'

From *Hare and Badger Go to Town* by Naomi Lewis and Tony Ross (Anderson Press).

Figure 10.6 Workshop 2, OHT 3

Discussion

The group will have some difficulty in completing the first set of words in Figure 10.4. The results will be much better for the second set of words in Figure 10.5.

The first letter of a word is far more helpful in generating the whole word than the middle letter is. Prompting children by giving the sound of the first letter helps them considerably to guess the word correctly. Letters inside words are far less helpful.

Activity 3: How first letter and context helps with unknown words

Put up Figure 10.6 and read this to the group, inviting parents to guess the words left out using the context and the first letter cue.

Discussion

The group will easily deduce the word from the context plus the first letter. They will already have guessed these as isolated words in the previous exercise. Invite parents to list reasons why this was the case. Could you make it easier for your child by asking questions which encourage them to think about the story, or to look more carefully at the text? For instance, where the child is unable to complete the final word in the sentence, '. . . we bring up our children p – – – – – – –.', despite the initial letter and context clues, the helper asks, '*How* do you think they brought up their children?'. This verbal cueing helps the child to develop an interrogative stance as well as promoting syntactic predictive skills, i.e. that the word which we are looking for is likely to be an adverb. For unknown adjectives the cue would be, 'What *sort* of inventions do humans come up with?'

This activity coming after the previous activity demonstrates the importance of focusing on the initial letter sound when reading unknown words. It also emphasises how important it is for children to understand the text they are reading. Children use grapho-phonic clues in their reading as well as the text before, and after, the word that they are making sense of.

In any activity it is important not to expose any one parent's efforts. Here simply ask, 'Has anyone got a word that fits?' Those parents lacking confidence and anxious about their child's reading may need encouragement and support about their own literacy skills. The parent who has 'forgotten his reading glasses' may be retaining personal dignity by concealing reading difficulties.

Home activity: story sequencing

Use the four 'stories' illustrated in Figure 10.7. Reproduce them and cut each into the six episodes. Put in envelopes and hand parents one story each.

Ask the parents to take the pictures home and, through discussion, to get their children to sort the pictures into a sequence that makes a coherent story. Discussions can begin by asking children to name the characters. Then they should be encouraged to tell the story from the pictures. Suggest to parents that they help children to expand the stories by asking, 'How did . . . feel in the story?' Again, the parents scribe their children's efforts.

Encourage parents to swap envelopes, as there are four stories in all. They need to scribe only one story each. Finished stories are sent back to the class teacher.

The stories illustrated here are most suitable for children of about six up to eight; at eight, more complete picture sequences may be required.

Workshop 3: Learning more about stories

This consists of text level activities. The purposes are:

- to begin to look at how children structure their writing;
- to look at the language which different kinds of story employ;
- to introduce the parents to shared reading;
- to look at the relationship between text and illustrations.

The resources needed are:

- completed stories from the last home activity;
- Workshop 3, OHT 1 (Figure 10.8); a copy of *Titch* by Pat Hutchins;
- Workshop 3, OHT 2 (Figure 10.9).

Figure 10.7 Home activity: sequencing of four stories

Story 2

Story 3

Story 4

Activity 1: Review of home activity

Read back some completed stories. Many parents will report that using the matchstick figures is a demanding task. Generally children enjoy the activity. It is interesting to note that many children make a perfectly viable coherent story, using a sequence that differs from the original. Story writing is a crucial aspect of children's developing literacy skills and this home activity can be used to introduce the approach used in school and to help parents to play a more directed role at home.

Activity 2: Structuring stories

In the National Curriculum, Year 2 children will be learning more about story structure than simply that stories have a beginning, a middle and an end. Analyse some of the stories from the home activity in Workshop 2 using the headings:

- main characters;
- problem or conflict;
- climax;
- resolution.

On an overhead projector demonstrate that the simple stories which the children and parents produced follow a predictable structure (Figure 10.8).

Use the matrix to analyse a short familiar text, e.g. *Titch* by Pat Hutchins.

The main parts of a story

1. *Main characters*. The characters are introduced and described. Titch is little. Mary is a bit bigger and Pete is a lot bigger.

2. *Problem or conflict*. Mary and Pete have big bikes; Titch has a tricycle. Mary and Pete have kites that fly high; Titch has a pinwheel.

3. *Climax*. Pete has a big spade. Mary has a fat flowerpot, but Titch has the tiny seed.

4. *Resolution*. The seed grows and grows and grows to be the biggest thing of all!

Figure 10.8 Workshop 3, OHT 1

Discussion

Any picture book can be analysed in this way. Extend the activity if there is time by discussing what kind of story this is. What previous knowledge or experience do the parents have of these characters and characters such as these? Why are children intrigued by even a very simple family story? What or whom do they identify with in the story?

Activity 3: Shared Reading

The teacher demonstrates reading strategies using a shared text. The class reads the text together and discusses ideas and textual features, engaging in a high level of interaction with the teacher.

This activity is an opportunity for the group leader to introduce or reinforce the notion of shared reading, which is a critical concept in the Literacy Hour. Put up Figure 10.9 and model the reading process by reading the text to the group. Demonstrate to the group the cues and strategies involved with the cloze passage and invite them to join in together as you point.

This summer has _____ the _____ since 1986. It's the _____ time inseven _____ that ___ _____ have had a _____ sun _____ without even _____ on holiday!

In fact, there were _____ when the _____ garden was _____ hot that I could only _____ out for _____ brief spell at _____ time. The _____ trouble was that the _____ all _____ up and _____ owing to _____ of water.

Figure 10.9 Workshop 3, OHT 2

Discussion

In the discussion, begin by explaining that you have chosen this particular passage to demonstrate shared reading. This is not a passage that you would necessarily be using with your class. Having read the passage with the group draw out the following points:

- What kind of text is this? (The answer is that it is direct speech; something said by a parent which has been written down. Look for the first person, 'I', which tells you that it is direct speech.)
- At what points did we read forward and then back before making our guess? This is a good strategy for correct guessing. We can encourage our children to use this method of finding unknown words.
- Did we correct our guesses in the light of further reading? For instance, how many people guessed 'worst' or 'best' in the first line in Figure 10.9, and then corrected to 'hottest' after further reading? Children may need help to do this.
- How does our knowledge of grammar help with our guesses? (This is because we expect

a subject, verb and object in each sentence. Demonstrate this with reference to the cloze activity.)

- Why does the last sentence slow us down? (The reason is that the difficulty level rises because so many key words are missing. The most helpful word is probably 'up'. The sentence should read: 'The worst trouble was the flowers all dried up and died owing to lack of water'.)
- Finally, the key in reading the passage was that most people have experienced a hot summer. This kind of writing is readily recognised and accessible. This made guessing easier.

Activity 4: Picture–text relationship

Hand out picture books to pairs of parents. Give them the opportunity to examine a book and to consider the extent to which the illustrations match the text. Use *Rosie's Walk* and *Come Away From the Water, Shirley,* to show how authors play with the text and picture relationship. Parents offer their views to the group and the point is made that children must be given full opportunity to read pictures as well as text.

Home activity: Analysing a simple text

This home activity aims to show how certain vocabulary and themes recur in particular children's books. Use the story structure in Figure 10.10, which can be photocopied and given to each participant.

Invite parents to analyse a book that they are reading with their children. The amount of support that parents give will depend on the individual child's needs. This activity has already been done in Workshop 2 and parents will, therefore, be familiar with it. If not, run through the activity briskly, using a favourite picture book. Easier texts that have worked well for this exercise include the following: *Come Away From the Water, Shirley*; *Mr Gumpie's Outing*; *Titch*; *Rosie's Walk*; *Peter's Chair*. Extended stories such as *Jim and the Beanstalk, The Shrinking of Treehorn* and *The Man Whose Mother Was a Pirate* also suit the activity.

The second part of the activity requires the parent and child to identify the *kind* of story that they are reading and to give reasons for their choice.

Look out for particular words and phrases in the book which are often in this kind of story and note them down. For example, in 'family stories', words would include brother, sister and neighbour. Fairy stories might include castle, knight and gnome. Sensitising parents and children to expected language helps with predictive skills.

Ask the parents to bring their efforts to the next workshop.

Our Story

- The main characters in the story were:

- The problem was:

- The climax of the story was :

- In the end:

Figure 10.10 Story structure

Workshop 4: Looking at stories and language; Looking at poetry

Workshop 4 consists of text level activities. The purposes are:

- to follow up on the home activity in Workshop 3 which looked at how stories were set out and explored in the language in certain sorts of stories;
- to introduce the group to poetry writing.

The resources are as follows:

- completed examples of home activity;
- examples of dictionaries used in school;
- some poetry books from the class or school library.

Activity 1: Follow up of the home activity in Workshop 3 (looking at story structure and the language of particular stories)

This is a follow-up discussion on the previous home activity where parents were asked in collaboration with their child to analyse the structure of a children's book. This may be thought a rather technical activity for the parent group and that they may be unfamiliar with the language. It is the language of the Literacy Hour and hopefully, therefore, not entirely new. This exercise can be viewed as reinforcing work that the school has already done with parents through Literacy Hour meetings.

In the discussion, examine any themes that books share. How easy was it to break the book down using the headings supplied? Could this lead to a writing activity?

With the group, examine the following questions:

- What types of story can the group identify from the books that the children are reading: adventure stories; fairy stories; family stories? Do they fit into the category of myths and legends, or parables and fables? How many overlap?
- Can the group find any words associated with particular types of story?

This activity gives parents further confidence and understanding about how stories work. When children understand the type of story that they are reading, their confidence and their ability to operate competently increase. Understanding how stories are told helps when children begin to write.

Activity 2: Introducing the group to writing poetry

Reading and writing poetry feature importantly in Key Stage 2. This poetry writing activity enables the class teacher to introduce some ideas and language which children will be experiencing in class and enables parents to talk more knowledgeably with their children about class activities.

The following points should be made in introducing the activity:

- Children are able to borrow poetry books from school.
- Parents should look out for poetry books to read to their children.
- Give parents a chance to see some examples in school. Their own enthusiasm will be shared by their children.
- Note the poetry in books such as We're Going on a Bear Hunt, where the child and the parent can chant together.

- Reading and writing poetry for pleasure are enjoyable family activities.
- A dictionary at home is important for all writing activities, especially poetry, where children will be searching for a precise and perhaps new word. Have dictionaries available for parents to look at.

Preferences

This particular activity is taken from Sandy Brownjohn's *Does It Have To Rhyme* (Hodder and Stoughton), which contains a wide range of poetry-writing ideas.

Divide the group into two teams. One team is the 'Hates', the other is the 'Loves'. Choose a subject which people react strongly to, such as cats, football or relatives. Arrange the teams opposite each other if the room allows and spend a little time preparing the group by discussing the chosen subject. Each take turns to shout to each other about the subject. The first member of the 'Loves' might shout, 'What I love about cats is their contented purr.' The first member of the 'Hates' might shout, 'What I hate about cats is the way that they howl at night.' Every member of the group has a turn. The leader scribes and reads out the resulting poems, 'Loves' first. The result is usually very amusing. Points to draw out are that poems do not necessarily rhyme and that this approach encourages us to think imaginatively about a subject in unusual and creative ways.

Home activity: Prepositions

(Introduce this activity by reading *Rosie's Walk* to the group.) This is a poetry game for parents and children to try out at home.

- Have some discussion about prepositions and distribute a list of these to each parent, e.g. under, through, next to, behind, above or over.
- Parent and child choose a subject, e.g. 'my window', 'the garden shed' or 'the broom cupboard', and take it in turns to write a line, always beginning with a preposition.
- These lines might be:
  - 'Inside the garden shed the silent spiders spin their webs.'
  - 'Over the garden shed, sparrows squabble.'
  - 'Through the front-room curtains, I peep at Auntie Kitty.'
  - 'Under the front room curtains, Dad's left shoe hides.'
- Other members of the family can contribute a line.
- The family writes down all the lines, producing a family poem, which children bring to school.
- A selection can be read out and displayed.

This activity widens the range of home activities and extends parental understanding of purposeful writing in school. Bring some examples to Workshop 5.

Workshop 5: Reading for a purpose

This considers text level activities. The purposes are:

- to review previous home activity;
- to explore the idea of comprehension and understanding;
- to look at reading for different purposes;
- to discover the value parents place on Caper activities.

The following resources are used:

- examples of the home poems;
- OHT 1 (Workshop 5) (Figure 10.11);
- OHT 2 (Workshop 5) (Figure 10.12);
- questionnaire.

Activity 1: Review of previous home activity

Read out some of the poems that children and parents have written. Discuss the wide range of ideas and how poetry helps creative and imaginative responses in writing. It is a form of writing which gives children (and hopefully their parents) immense pleasure. Poems are a personal response and unusual and thoughtful ideas are rewarded. Poems can also be very short. This is important when it comes to drafting and redrafting.

Activity 2: Reading for meaning

Comprehension is all about reading for meaning. An effective reader is able to read accurately, fluently and with understanding, to understand and respond to the text being read, and to read, analyse and evaluate a wide range of texts, including literature from the English literary heritage and from other cultures and traditions (*Revised National Curriculum for English in England and Wales, General Requirements for English 1995*).

A tangled snarl

The Gribble strigged the blue black Dorigg into a drewish set of Taygon.

Shaking off the Taygon the Dorigg frassed the Gribble with its mighty blawk.

In the end both the Gribble, with its croving strigger, and the blue-black Dorigg were exhausted by the effort of it all. They embraced and agreed that it had been a good crimble.

Figure 10.11 Workshop 5, OHT 1

The passage in Figure 10.11 is put up on the overhead projector. The purpose of the activity is to demonstrate how the 'correct' answer can be given without really understanding the text.

Read the passage aloud, with expression, and then ask the parents the following eight questions:

- What colour was the Dorigg?
- What did the Gribble do to the Dorigg?
- How did the Dorigg get rid of the Taygon?
- What did the Dorigg use to frass the Gribble?
- What word did the writer use to describe the Dorigg's strigger?
- How did they both feel at the end of it all?
- What did they do to make you think that they had finished as friends?
- Why do you think that they thought that it had been a good crimble?

The group answers the questions more or less correctly and may conclude that this shows that they understand and comprehend the passage. Accept their response and then introduce the two following essay titles, which, of course, the text does not help with at all: Give a Gribble's eye view of the Dorigg, *or* how would a Dorigg cope in a world without Gribbles?

It is possible to answer the comprehension questions at a surface or 'literal' level, without a full understanding of the text. Discuss the need for effective listening with fluent readers and how questioning can encourage children to think more about what they are reading. There will be occasions when children will be reading with only superficial understanding. This will be true even with apparently fluent readers who may be galloping through text to little purpose. The attention of an interested adult can facilitate an exploration of any ambiguities or uncertainties that the child experiences when reading.

Activity 3: Reading for different purposes – some key terms

This activity develops the notion of reading for different purposes (Figure 10.12). Some key terms and activities are introduced which their children will meet during National Curriculum Years 2 and 3. The key terms are printed in italics and explanations of them given below. It is not intended that the terms should be introduced to the parent group. The idea, again, is to give parents a taster of the language and thinking involved in the Literacy Hour.

Read the recipe chorally with the group and ask each of the questions below:

- What are the ingredients in the recipe? (The reader is able to give a correct answer by looking at the text and not know what the story is about. Requires a surface or *literal* understanding of the text.)
- Why is there a warning in the last sentence? (You have to think about this, using your own personal experience and knowledge to answer the question, i.e. on its own the soup is not an adequate source of food. Requires *deductive* understanding.)
- Why is this called a 'fat burning diet'? (You have to read between the lines in order to get the answer. In language of the Literacy Strategy this requires an *inferential* response.)
- Will this diet work? (This requires the reader to weigh evidence and to make judgements. The reader makes an *evaluation*.)
- How did you read the recipe?
  Did you read it very quickly? This is called *skimming*.
  When you saw the questions, did you read through it again quickly, this time looking out for a particular detail? This is called *scanning*.

Basic fat-burning soup

Ingredients

6 large onions

1 or 2 cans of tomatoes

1 large head of cabbage

2 green peppers

1 bunch of celery

1 packet of onion
soup mix

Season with salt, pepper, curry and parsley if desired or bouillon (4 cubes) or hot sauce.

Cut the vegetables in small to medium pieces and cover with water. Boil fast for 10 minutes. Reduce to simmer and continue to cook until the vegetables are tender. This soup can be eaten whenever you are hungry. Eat as much as you want, whenever you want. This soup will not add calories. The more you eat, the more you will lose. Fill a Thermos in the morning if you will be away during the day. If eaten alone for indefinite periods, you could suffer malnutrition.

Figure 10.12 Workshop 5, OHT 2

Were there any parts which you read very carefully? You would probably need to do this as you were preparing the recipe. This is called *detailed* reading.
- What kind of writing is this – fiction, map, instructional or informational? It is instructional although many participants might see it as largely fiction!

This activity usually generates much discussion. You will need to move on briskly to the next activity, which is an opportunity for the group to comment on the year's workshops and any other related events.

Activity 3: Feedback on the year's activities

This is the last workshop of the year and is the opportunity for the group to give their views. Find out from the group which workshop activity they found most useful and what activities in the year they participated in.

If you wish, distribute the questionnaire given in Figure 10.13.

The completed questionnaires can be used to assess overall reaction, to gain feedback and to make improvements on the project.

Parent questionnaire

Please tick those activities which you have tried this year.

First meeting _____ Workshops _____

Reading clinics_____ Other events _____

Which of the above have you found the most useful?

_____

Please tick the appropriate boxes.

	Not at all	A little bit	A great deal
The project has helped my child with reading.	☐	☐	☐
We spend more time reading together.	☐	☐	☐
I know more about children's books.	☐	☐	☐
My attitude to reading has changed.	☐	☐	☐
As a family we are reading more.	☐	☐	☐

The most important thing for me has been

_____

How many books do you think that your child has read this year?   10–20, 20–30, 30–40, 40+

Would you like to see this scheme extended next year? Yes/No

Name of parent: _____

Parent of: _____

Figure 10.13 Parent questionnaire

Workshop games

The following games can be used as 'warm-up' activities for workshops. Anyone introducing these games into a workshop needs to have practised them beforehand. Parents can use all these language games at home.

Going on a picnic

The group sits in a circle. The leader begins with, 'My name is _____. I'm going on a picnic today. I'm taking _____.'

The item must begin with the same letter as the speaker's name, e.g. *Melanie ... a melon ... marmite sandwiches.* The leader concludes, 'And I can join the picnic.'

Passing around the circle, each person gives their first name and the item that they are going to bring. Those making the name and the item link can come on the picnic. Those who do not make the link are told regretfully they cannot come. By the end of the game each parent has been introduced to everyone else. Make sure the game ends before those left out of the picnic begin to feel uncomfortable. Never finish with a few anxious parents left outside the 'secret'.

Pass the buck

The 'buck' can be a paper ball or a soft toy. The group sits in a circle. The teacher explains: 'The buck is passed around the group. If it comes to you, you must speak until I clap my hands. You then pass the buck to anyone you can reach, in any direction. You must not throw it.'

This is an elimination game, i.e. anyone who dries up while they are holding the buck loses a life. All players begin with three lives.

To begin with, make the speaking intervals very brief but, once the group has practised the game, vary the intervals and start to eliminate the non-speakers.

At some point it may be necessary to introduce a 'no repetition' rule.

Random sentences

For this game you need one pack of letter cards. Each parent is given two small paper circles to act as full stops. The aim is to create a sentence, however foolish.

The games moves clockwise. The opening player turns up a card from the pack on the table and says a word beginning with the letter on the card. The next player then turns up a card and has to say a word beginning with that letter which could conceivably fit with the first word, and so on round the table. The words must make sense! If a player gets stuck, they can use a full stop. Once the full stops have been used up, if players are stuck for a word, they are out of the game. Letters Q and Z are 'wild'.

Chinese whispers

The group sits in a circle. The leader whispers a sentence into the ear of the person next to them. The whisper is passed around the circle. Once the whisper returns to the point of origin, retrace its course with each person stating what she or he heard. Close the session with a reading from *The Surprise Party* by Pat Hutchins (Picture Puffin), a book based on the same idea.

The preposition party

The group sits in a circle. The following prepositions are written on the overhead projector or the board:

before	around	under
behind	over	at
beside	above	against

Each player in turn begins a sentence with one of these prepositions and each sentence has to continue the story, with the last sentence finishing it off. Each player has three lives. This game is used with the last workshop of the Caper year as it is much more demanding than the others.

CHAPTER 11
Volunteer helpers in school

Workshops and clinics highlight the enthusiasts among the parent group and those who may have some spare time to help within the school on a voluntary basis. This further links the parents with school and provides an excellent resource for the class teacher to draw on. Volunteers can be particularly helpful in supporting the handful of children whose parents do not involve themselves in the project. For this group of children the listening group provides extra in-school listening support.

Schools must have a policy on volunteers. Their contribution needs to be carefully negotiated and agreed. While they are in school, volunteers need to be purposefully and actively engaged and their work monitored. Volunteers should only be permitted to read with children while a teacher is present, because they are not trained, as such, and they will not have been cleared, as all teachers must be, to work unsupervised with children. They must be welcomed in school and recognised as having what has been called 'equivalent expertise' (Wolfendale 1992). They may not be trained teachers but bring to school their own experience and understanding of how children learn.

Volunteers will be largely involved in hearing children read, but the lesson learnt from the clinics and workshops is that, if it is done properly, this is far from a straightforward task. The volunteers need to be aware of the ground rules of working in the school and be provided with initial training in active listening. The way that adults listen needs to reflect the school's approach to the teaching of reading. Listening performance requires supportive monitoring and the teacher doing this will find the advice in the section on Caper Clinics invaluable.

The would-be volunteers are met as a group by the head teacher or the class teacher, who stresses the need for confidentiality concerning the reading performance of individual children. To engage the parents in a successful listening group, it is emphasised that their commitment must be regular, reliable and sustained throughout the year. A small sustained commitment is preferable to one which is inconsistent or erratic. Those parents still interested in forming such a group are organised into a timetable, usually of hour-long sessions. One hour a day forms a realistic limit to enthusiastic listening and offers minimum disruption and maximum benefit to the class. A task board helps to ensure that volunteers understand what is required of them during the hour.

Sample listening timetable

A letter along the lines of that given in Figure 11.1 should be sent to each parent in the group.

Note that the contact point for making any adjustments to the timetable is, in fact, a parent, as this adds to the group's sense of responsibility.

As suggested earlier, many volunteers will already have attended initial meetings, workshops or clinic sessions. Some may have attended a local authority course. It is still a good idea to organise a short training session for volunteer helpers to overcome any initial apprehensions about working in school. This can be undertaken by school staff but is also delivered in some local education authorities by the literacy coordinator. Training adds to the status of the activity and conveys to the volunteer the value which the school attaches to it.

Dear   ,

As agreed, the parents' listening timetable will begin each day at _____ and last for about 1 hour.

Please check that the information shown is correct.

Monday   Tuesday   Wednesday   Thursday   Friday

If there are any problems about coming in, please contact _____ (name of parent coordinator).

Thanks once again for your support. We look forward to seeing you throughout the year.

Yours sincerely

Figure 11.1 Letter to parents confirming volunteer time

Training is designed to reinforce the Caper message that reading is fun and volunteers are asked:

- to accept the children's attempts at reading;
- to avoid a skills approach to listening;
- to convey their own sense of excitement and enthusiasm for the stories;
- to praise the readers too much rather than too little.

The following four-stage model for listeners, designed by teachers, has been used successfully in a number of schools.

Stage model for listeners

The stages are as follows:

- *Stage 1* is where the young readers know only words they have seen in a familiar context. The strategy is to *talk* about the picture with the child, to *say* the word and allow the child to *repeat* it, and then to *praise* his or her success.
- *Stage 2* is where the young readers guess at words from what they know about how language works, and do not relate sounds to letter shapes. The strategy is to *give* the word and to *read* the sentence; the child then *re-reads* it.
- *Stage 3* is where children seem to be uncertain about the word because of sound or letter confusion. The strategy is to *say* the word, to *clue* the word or to *cue* the word. To *clue* the word the listener might ask what word it might be. The child can be given a *cue* by being told the first sound in the word.
- *Stage 4* is where the child is attempting to read for meaning and knows about letter–sound relationship. A child at this stage is developing his or her own cues and clues. The strategy is to *re-read* up to the 'stuck' word, then to miss it out and to *read on* past the 'stuck' word to the end of the sentence. Ask the child to *guess* back at the missing word.

Parents need to be introduced gradually to this four-stage model until they can move freely between stages to adjust to each child.

There are many obvious limits to the model, but it provides a relatively simple and structured approach to listening and a fairly concise starting point for the parents in the listening group. The best indicator of their success as listeners is the children's eagerness to take up the opportunity to read to them.

From time to time a teacher must monitor the work of each volunteer. Without this support the volunteer may revert to passive listening or unsystematic phonic cueing. Whilst most parents are engaged in listening within the classroom itself, some schools have widened the brief of volunteers to support group work within the Literacy Hour.

Sometimes schools have elected the library as the setting in which volunteers can help. This requires a more structured arrangement for supervision and monitoring to ensure that the work done dovetails with what is happening in the classroom and that volunteers are continuing to listen purposefully and actively.

Within the school, parental involvement of this kind is increasingly popular with schools, and effective. Some parents have stayed on to help the teacher in successive years after their own child has moved on to another class.

CHAPTER 12

Caper with nursery and reception age children

The early years are a vital time in developing a child's language and thought processes. Written language promotes more complex thought and enables ways of expression which are not available in oral language on its own. Caper, in securing daily child–parent reading, enhances the process.

For the early years, some modifications need to be made to the scheme because of the different stage children are at in their development, their greater dependency upon adult help and the different interests they demonstrate. For schools this is a critical stage in the partnership with parents, for whom this may be the first contact they have had with school or teachers since they themselves were children. Impressions laid down at this point are long lasting.

During the early years, schools:

- help steer parents towards books and authors that work;
- guide on the most helpful ways of drawing children into books;
- reassure and advise parents who may have concerns about their child's development;
- establish a regular reading habit at home which only works properly in partnership with a child's parent.

Aims for younger children

Where the scheme begins with younger children the aims might differ in some respects and the following desirable outcomes were generated in discussion by a group of early-years teachers about to start a scheme in their schools:

- to extend children's oral language skills by improving language comprehension, augmenting their vocabulary and increasing their picture recognition skills;
- to promote children's interest in both picture and story books by changing children's book use behaviour, by increasing the frequency of book usage and by changing children's attitudes towards the use and care of books;
- to develop children's concepts about print by increasing their 'pre-reading' skills;
- to change parental behaviour by increasing the time that they spend in sharing books with their very young children;
- to improve home–school links by increasing parent–teacher contact and thus developing positive parent attitudes towards their children's schools;

In the previous example, teachers indicated not only desired outcomes but also how they intended to bring them about.

The key point is that each school should develop its own aims, objectives and operational plan. In each case these are likely to be unique to that school's needs and context.

Initial meeting with parents

An invitation, using letter 1 (Figure 4.1) and letter 2 (Figure 4.2), can be issued. Letter 3 (Figure 4.3), for those parents who missed the meeting, should omit the reference in the second paragraph to helping when a child 'gets stuck on a word'.

Attendance will be improved if, in addition to the letter, a poster advertising the meeting is displayed.

Parents are generally asked to stay on after they have delivered their children, or to come in half an hour earlier. Space permitting, meetings can be held in one part of the classroom while the children are in another part, supervised by the nursery assistant.

The 'model talk' for parents of this group of children has been written to engage children as well. It will, therefore, work just as well if parents and children are sitting together. (If only infant chairs are available, the speaker must be sure to use an infant-sized chair as well. Everyone quickly becomes accustomed to them.)

For this talk, an overhead projector and a supply of good books, suitable for this age group, should be available. As parents arrive, they should be given one of the books to look at. Do not start the scheme immediately after the meeting. Hand out the Daily Comment Booklets the following Monday and collect them in the following Friday. It is worth reassuring parents that, although the booklet is to be kept carefully and is important evidence of their children's development, it can be replaced if it gets lost.

Model talk for parents of three- to five-year-olds

Informal links between parents and teachers of this group of children are generally stronger than with older pupils. A formal introduction by the head teacher is, therefore, not regarded as quite as important to the scheme's initiation. However, a welcome by the head teacher adds to the scheme's credibility and helps to establish it as an important new development in school.

Head teacher's introduction (five minutes)

The importance of reading

It is impossible to exaggerate the importance of reading. All school subjects require it. If you cannot read labels, instructions, or street signs, you really are at a disadvantage. We also know that children who read well are more likely to do well in school. The best predictor of future academic success is reading age at 7 (Figure 12.1).

> # Children who read well
> # do well in school

Figure 12.1 Early years, OHT 1

Parents can help

We know that 60% of parents help with reading. Research shows that the best and most effective help that parents can give is to read to their children regularly and, as they grow older, to listen to them read aloud every day (Figure 12.2).

> # . 60% of parents
> # help with reading

Figure 12.2 Early years, OHT 2

What is reading?

Reading is a complex skill (Figure 12.3). Let us see whether we can make sense of this strange writing. This must be what it is like to a child coming to reading for the first time. Does the picture help? Come on class you're not really trying are you!

Figure 12.3 Early years, OHT 3; mystery script [Dad has the ball./"Come and play, Sally."/ Sally holds the ball./"I can play ball well,"/she says.]

The _____ that my eldest _____ started at the

_____ school was one of the _____ days of

_____ life. She seemed excited _____ the way

_____ to the school but, once _____ the play-

ground, she went quiet.

The _____ rang; so I _____ her to her _____

teacher. As soon as _____ let _____, she burst

_____ tears. I felt terrible; the _____ wanted

_____ to _____ but I couldn't leave _____

like _____.

Figure 12.4 Early years, OHT 4; guessing the missing words

What were our reading strategies?

We guess at print.	It is acceptable for children to guess.
We needed several attempts to get the unknown word.	Our children may need a little extra time to grasp the word.
We leave out unknown words and guess back at them.	Children may need to be shown that this is acceptable when reading.
We change our guesses in the light of further reading.	If children guess, we need to encourage them to refine their guessing sense.
For *us*, the 'right word' is one that makes sense.	If our children make an occasional error, we should not make them sacrifice the flow of story for precision.

Figure 12.5 Early years, OHT 5

Help the group to solve the puzzle after they have struggled for a while. The points to bring out are:

- Pointing helps the child to learn that reading goes from left to right.
- Looking at books together is supposed to be fun.
- Guessing is important.
- The illustration is important in making sense of the story.
- What skills do we use? (Figure 12.4)

Let us look at this passage and try to fill in the missing words. You read while I point How were we able to read the missing words? (Figure 12.5)

Let me read it you.

How do children learn to read?

They learn through repetition. Children see words around them everywhere. They see their names and they get to know favourite words such as mum, dad, teddy, cat and milk. Children will come across words repeated often in the books that you read to them. Through this process of repetition, children develop what is called a sight vocabulary, i.e. words that they can recognise automatically.

They learn through phonics or sounding out. This is an important skill for children to learn. It helps them work out words which they are not sure of or have not seen before. However, sounding out can be tricky, so our advice to parents is (Figure 12.6): do not let children struggle over words which they do not know. Give them the word and get on with the story.

Do not let children struggle over words which they do not know. Give them the word and get on with the story.

Figure 12.6 Early years, OHT 6

What is Caper?

Caper is a simple scheme which helps you to help your child enjoy reading. We are asking you to read with your child for not more than twenty minutes each day.

Books in the scheme

A good supply of books is available. You and your child will select a book, take it home and read it together. Then you can change it.

Daily Comment Booklet

This is to be taken home by the parent and filled in each week: it is then brought back to school. The teacher will acknowledge it and make appropriate comments.

This record helps:

- to keep a written account of books read and the response of child and parent;
- to foster the scheme;
- to promote good home–school links.

Class teacher's talk (20 minutes)

The aim is to give guidance on how parents should help children to enjoy books. Begin by projecting a cloze exercise on to a wall or screen. Any passage from a children's book will do, with one word in five deleted. The cloze passage in Figure 12.4, recorded in conversation with a parent, will work very well.

Ask your group to read out the passage together as you point to each word. This is usually quite an amusing exercise as the group guesses at the missing words. The purpose of the exercise is to demonstrate to parents that the processes which they use when reading are very much like those used by children.

Central to the exercise is the importance of 'hypothesis making' in the development of reading (Payton 1984). The points to bring out, therefore, are these:

- *We guess when we are reading.* Children are listening and guessing as we read to them. They hear the beginning of the sentence. They often guess its ending before we read it, and *check* what we have read with their guess. Surprise comes when the check and the guess do not match. Encourage guessing by leaving out the *occasional* word for your child to 'fill in'.
- *Our guess is better if we can remember what came earlier in the story.* Children's understanding is helped if we remind them *occasionally* of what has happened previously in the story. This is especially important in longer stories not finished in one sitting. (Refer here, if necessary, to serials or the weekly soap opera and the practice of 'recap'.)
- *Pointing at the words can make it more difficult to read with 'meaning'.* (If necessary, read again through the cloze passage, with exaggerated and delayed pointing at each word and deletion.) For young children, pointing is important because it focuses attention on words, helps develop the left to right rule of written language and shows children that there is a link between what is said and what is written. Children, however, respond to and will have a good grasp of the rhythms of language. Make sure that you read to them with appropriate dramatic emphasis.

At this point in the talk, select two or three books to read to the group. Books that work very well for this exercise are the following:

John Brown, Rose and the Midnight Cat by Jenny Wagner (Puffin Books): the eternal triangle involving an old lady, her dog John Brown and the Midnight Cat;
Jim and the Beanstalk by Raymond Briggs (Puffin Books): this is an extremely funny sequel to the traditional tale that everyone knows;
Rosie's Walk by Pat Hutchins (Bodley Head);
Peter's Chair by Ezra Jack Keats (Bodley Head): a brilliant account of the jealousy caused by the arrival of a new baby and how it is resolved.

Teachers will have their own favourites which will work equally well. Ten key points to be drawn from the selected reading are given below.

Key points

1. The most compelling part of a book is what happens next! In any book, tensions set up are resolved in one way or another, although some books end on a further question mark, e.g. 'The wicked wolf was never seen again . . . for a long time.' Therefore, there should not be too many interruptions or too much quizzing by the parent during the reading. Begin by apologising for breaking this rule in the talk! You have to do this to illustrate the points that you are going to make.
2. Make sure that you and your child are sitting comfortably, side by side, so that both of you can see the book.
3. Bedtime is *not* always a good time. Children are usually tired. It is also a *busy* time of day. After tea, or when a younger baby has been put to bed, may be better.
4. For some families breakfast time is a good opportunity for reading. It is important to accustom children to the *language of books*, e.g. title, author, illustrator, chapter and 'dedicated to'. These words should be introduced naturally as they arise.
5. Illustrations help children to understand what is happening or may happen in the story. Reading the picture, the way in which picture and text link, is a skill that children need to learn. Allow children to look at the picture before reading the text. The horizontal tear of the page is the tell-tale sign of a parent trying to turn the page while the child's finger is still firmly holding it down! Do *not* use the illustrations to 'teach' ('What colour are the trees?' or 'How many boats can you see?'). This spoils the flow of the story and interrupts a child's enjoyment of it.
6. Encourage your child to guess on occasion as you read, trying not to spoil the story. Guessing promotes the child's active participation. When a child is not guessing correctly, it may be that the book is failing to engage the child, because of its content.
7. Just as adults may find a book uninviting or boring, children often react in a similar way and it is important to be sensitive to their apparent reluctance to read. When a child is unhappy with a book, the parent should change it, noting in the comment booklet *why* that particular book did not work. Caper is partly about children learning to choose books, and making mistakes about what you like is an important part of this learning process.
8. It is important to encourage active engagement in the text by asking your child what they think may happen next in the story. Examine the clues in the text or in the illustrations which might have helped in making this prediction. When you arrive at the last page of the book, ask your child to guess the ending. This allows them to check with their earlier prediction. In some stories the ending may just be a 'one liner', e.g. in *Where the Wild Things Are* 'and it was still hot!'
9. After you have read the story, try to talk to your child about it. Did they like it? Was it like any others they know? Would they like it again? Their comments can be entered in the comment booklet.
10. Children will very often, quite spontaneously retell stories which have been read to them. They should be encouraged to do this. Retelling stories has a very positive effect on children's language development (Wade 1984).

The talk ends with a recap of the points made in it. It is very helpful in doing so to produce a modified version of the Caper Guidance Booklet (p. 114), taking out any references to hearing children read since, for most parents of this age group, reading to children will be the primary activity. The Guidance Booklet will remind parents of the scheme's purpose and will also give them support in explaining the scheme to other people at home unable to come. There may be some schools where parents might appropriately be asked to introduce the scheme to parents who did not attend. The Guidance Booklet helps them to do this.

The meeting should be ended by thanking parents for coming.

Clinic sessions for the early years

Caper clinic sessions will prove worthwhile with the one or two parents who fail to make the group meetings. It is also important to stress that any parent present at the initial meeting who wishes to be seen individually for advice or support needs only to ask. There may be some parents who are convinced that their child is not progressing normally, or perhaps one or two who may lack the confidence to join in fully with the scheme.

Workshops for early-years parents

These are not as formal as in the scheme for six- to eight-year-olds but are nevertheless vital in maintaining the scheme's momentum and developing parents' and children's commitment. They represent an opportunity to gain feedback from parents and to suggest additional activities to them. Parent workshops can be held once or twice a term in order to maintain parental interest. Activities can be selected from the workshops aimed at parents of older children. Discussion of parents' comments in the Caper Comment Booklet, particularly about books that have worked and the reasons why they were successful, can be included as a workshop activity. Other activities at home can include illustrating books that children have and retelling stories which parents record and bring to the group. One workshop can focus on reading poetry together and reading a favourite book to other parents. The list of activities is extensive and, as parents meet, further ideas will be generated and can be followed up either at home or by the teacher in school (Figure 12.7). Activities at home have included poster and collage competitions where the subject is a favourite story or incident in a story. There are also very good and reasonably priced videos, which could be discussed and shared. For example, Richard Scarry's excellent videos (try the *Best ABC Video* and the *Best Learning Songs Video Ever)* and Eric Carle's video versions of *The Very Hungry Caterpillar*, *The Mixed-Up Chameleon* and *The Very Quiet Cricket*).

The 'Caper Corner'

Parents are invited into school to choose books with their children. Most teachers will find that this works best if the books to be borrowed are available close to, but not actually in, the classroom. This can be a corridor space, but it is all the better if a recessed area is available where parents and children can choose without feeling pressured. Books should, of course, be

Getting the most from a favourite story

1   Read the whole story.

2   Read it often.

3   Talk about the pictures and the story.

4   Use your finger to point to the text as you read it.

5   Once your child is familiar with the story omit the last words in key sentences. (Your child will supply the words.)

6   Move on to leaving out key phrases for your child to respond.

7   The child will soon 'read' the book from memory.

8   Give them the chance to show this skill to a favourite adult.

9   Return to such favourite stories to re-experience succes whenever reading together loses momentum.

Figure 12.7

well displayed and not presented 'spine on'. A good supply of books is an absolute must. The walls of the 'Caper corner' can be used to display Caper-related activity, an up-to-date list of the top 20 books and so on. Parents are often willing to volunteer as 'library helpers'; one job might be to help with the wall display.

CHAPTER 13
Caper chain

These links are essential to maintain the momentum of the project, whatever age group is involved.

Newsletters

These perform the key function of reminding parents that the project is ongoing and that they have made a commitment to it. They are best used at the beginning of a new term or just after half-term, when parents' enthusiasm may need to be rekindled.

The example of a newsletter shown in Figure 13.1 was published after the Caper questionnaire was returned from parents. Their replies provided the information for the questionnaire. This particular school chose Pacer (Parents and Children Enjoying Reading) as their acronym.

If you are lucky enough to have access to a scanner, why not include children's work and illustrations. Further examples of newsletters which schools have sent out using graphics to promote the project are given in Figure 13.2.

Graphics

There are any number of fonts available which can be used to improve the quality of communication between home and school and used specifically in newsletters or information sheets (Figures 13.3–13.6).

Parents and Children Enjoying Reading
NEWSLETTER   Perivale Primary School
Spring Term 1998

Pacer this year

Last year the project started with Year 1 children. This year ,Year 1 and Year 2 children will have the chance to participate. We have made a bit of a late start but everyone is as enthusiastic as ever.

We shall start off with a meeting the details of which are included with this Newsletter.

As last year there will be a Comment Booklet and your child will be able to bring home a new book regularly.

Last year

Thank you to those parents who returned the questionnaires. They will be very helpful in running the scheme again this year. Your views are summarised below.

What the teachers thought

The teachers were all very enthusiastic and expressed the view that the PACER project had made a real difference to every child's reading progress.

What the parents said

Not all parents attended the meeting at the beginning of the project, but all parents were contacted and received a copy of the Perivale Reading Booklet

In the questionnaire, 60% of parents said that they read to their child every day and 30% every other day. So well done to those parents!

Nearly all parents completed the Comment Booklet. They realised just how well this enabled them to keep in touch with school.

Parents said that they were delighted with the books that their children brought home.

Lots of people at home helped with reading, including mothers, fathers, grandparents, brothers and sisters. Very positive comments were made by parents about the project.

Your comments

'It has encouraged my daughter to read more books and to look forward to going to the Library.'

'A regular supply of new books encourages my daughter to read more.'

'I consider the reading booklet a useful source of information. I feel that a workshop would have been beneficial.'

'She always liked books, but this scheme has improved her reading.'

'It made me aware of the difficulties that a child has when learning to read and therefore I am more patient and tolerant.'

'It helps because the teacher is involved and they check the comments regularly. It helps me to check on my child's competence and capability.'

Last but not least

Have you got what it takes to be a volunteer? We need volunteers to help with reading in school. A couple of hours a week will make a big difference to children's reading. Training will be provided; so come on!

Figure 13.1 Newsletter, Perivale Primary School

Figure 13.2 Examples of other newsletters

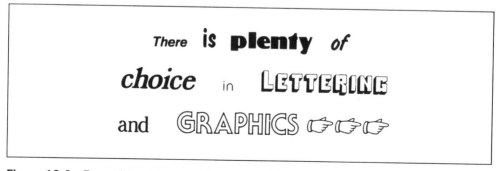

Figure 13.3 Examples of different fonts available

Figure 13.4   Newsletter graphics

Figure 13.5 Memory joggers

Figure 13.6 Workshop graphics

CHAPTER 14

Evaluating the Caper scheme—has it worked?

Teachers will want to know whether the Caper scheme has been worthwhile and will therefore wish to carry out some kind of evaluation.

Such an evaluation will help to decide:

- whether to continue with the scheme
- whether other teachers could introduce the scheme in school, in particular those teachers to whom children already involved in the scheme will be moving the following September.

An evaluation of the scheme will give the feedback needed to tell whether the extra effort demanded has paid off. Furthermore, an evaluation provides very useful information for governors and parents. Teachers in Caper are urged to use a newsletter, posters or letters home to let parents know, as a group, how the scheme is progressing. This is a recognition of the vital role that parents play in the scheme and the contribution which they are making to it. Feedback to parents will help to maintain and develop the Caper scheme.

What is measured at the evaluation stage is determined almost entirely by the aims of the scheme, and readers will recall that the very first step in initiating Caper was to draw up, preferably with other teachers (why not parents as well?), the targets of their own school or class scheme.

Let us assume that the following were the aims selected. For each aim, methods of measurement can be suggested as follows.

Aim

To promote the reading levels of children involved in the scheme.

How to measure

Assess the reading levels of children at the beginning and end of each year. Reading quotients for project pupils should rise following the scheme. Reading quotients are given in most reading tests. Otherwise they can be easily calculated using the following formula:

$$\frac{\text{reading age}}{\text{chronological age}} \times \frac{100}{1}$$

At the end of 12 months and without any kind of added intervention, one would expect about one third of a retested group to have a reading quotient more or less the same, one third a reading quotient higher than when first tested, and one third a lower reading quotient. Any significant change to this normal statistical variation suggests that school-based factors are operating.

Tests of reading vary. Most schools now use tests which assess comprehension skills as well as the more traditional 'word recognition' skills. Caper enhances both sets of skills, but particularly the former. Teachers can therefore expect particular gains in comprehension skills.

Aim

To promote language skills.

How to measure

It is possible to obtain an objective measure of improvement in the area of language comprehension.

The *British Picture Vocabulary Scale* (2nd edn) measures the receptive vocabulary of 3.0- to 15.08-year-olds and is available from NFER–Nelson Publishing Company, Darville House, 2 Oxford Road East, Windsor, Berkshire, SL4 1DF.

It is a simple test to administer and interpret and is ideal for assessing the comprehension skills of children for whom English is an additional language. This test can be given at the beginning and at the end of the first year.

Aim

To foster positive attitudes towards reading.

How to measure

Use the appropriate children's reading attitude scale especially produced for this purpose. There are scales for different age and ability groups. Ideally these should be administered at the beginning and the end of the Caper year. The scales can be found on pp. 128–32.

Aim

To develop positive parental attitudes towards school.

How to measure

Check on this through the Daily Comment Booklet, or in the parental questionnaires, which can be found on pp. 126–7. Do try to use these questionnaires or something like them. They provide invaluable feedback from parents and enable you in turn to let parents know as a group how Caper is going. You will be surprised and delighted by the feedback that parents provide.

Aim

To extend parents' and teachers' knowledge and experience of good literature for children.

How to measure

Note the growing sophistication in the remarks that parents make about their children's reading in the Comment Booklets. Working with parents and in such an intensive scheme teachers also find that their knowledge and skills have extended. Everyone involved in the Caper scheme finds out a great deal more about children's books.

Aim

To extend children's experience of books.

How to measure

Check the number of books that children are reading in a week or a month. Ask a colleague whose class is not yet involved in Caper to carry out a similar check. The sheer volume of books that children in the scheme get through has astonished teachers. Try not to request parents to 'hear page 26', or to use a page-number bookmark. This would be to stress that learning to read is about the amount that you read and not about an imaginative response to text. Children are, however, quite happy to keep a record of the books that they read. Remember, when checking the number of books read, that Caper encourages the re-reading of favourite books.

Critical incident diary

As the project develops, teachers will notice particular incidents which may help other staff to decide whether to embark upon Caper. These might include ideas for improving the approach to parents, a child's reaction to a particular book, or suggestions for the next newsletter to parents. It is suggested that each teacher in Caper keeps a 'Critical incident diary'. This should be used to record important incidents which might otherwise be forgotten and provide valuable evidence in weighing up the positives and negatives.

Table 14.1 Caper profiles

Name	Reading age in September	Reading age in June	Attitude to reading*	Number of books read	Questionnaire 1 returned	Questionnaire 2 returned	Use of Comment Booklet**
Robert Seago	6.4	7.6	4	32	Yes	Yes	3
Jaspreet Ali	6.3	7.1	3	24	Yes	No	2
Mary Conlon	5.9	7.1	4	27	Yes	Yes	5

* = 1, never uses books unless told to; 5, always in a book.
** = 1, Comment Booklet rarely returned; 5, Comment Booklet always returned

Caper profiles

The Caper profiles in Table 14.1 give teachers an overall view of the pattern of Caper activity in their classrooms and are a quick way of reviewing the level of involvement of individual children.

CHAPTER 15
Conclusion

The National Literacy Hour introduced throughout the UK from September 1998 will impinge dramatically on classroom practice. Some will argue that it represents a 'dumbing down', in that the best practice is already well in advance of what is being advocated. Furthermore, one has heard it suggested that the programmes are overdetermined and inflexible and will discourage teachers from thinking creatively. The shift towards the class teaching of literacy explicit in the strategy will make it harder to extend the more able and to deliver individual education plans for children with special educational needs.

In fact the Literacy Task Force found widespread support for the approach in the strategy which is based firmly on successful educational practice and provides detailed practical guidance which teachers have welcomed. Teachers accede to a need for additional training, recognised as effective on a national level, which updates their skills. They welcome the Literacy Strategy and its commitment at all levels to raise children's written language abilities. The *National Literacy Strategy – Framework for Teaching* (Department for Education and Employment 1998b) describes in detail the teaching objectives to enable Reception to Year 6 children to become literate. Schools have also been supplied with detailed guidance on the implementation of the Literacy Hour. Many have been aware of the need for a more directed and targeted teaching of written language skills – one which moves beyond the current focus on the class reading scheme.

Teachers readily concede that the demands of the National Curriculum have meant that hearing children read is no longer a feature of classroom practice. Listening to children read irregularly and briefly has little effect upon reading attainment (Southgate *et al.* 1981). Southgate *et al.* found that teachers in their sample working with seven- to eight-year-olds listened to them read individually for two–three minutes each day. This pattern of teacher listening may be different in the early years, but teachers recognise that there simply is not enough time to hear children read for long enough, often enough. The implication in the Literacy Project is that parents can and do give this support and need encouragement, support and training from school to undertake the task more effectively.

The major change as far as reading is concerned is that parents are at last officially recognised as essential contributors to the wider educational project. Schools cannot do it all (not that they ever did!) and parental involvement is regarded as a *key priority* in the National Literacy Strategy. All teachers have been reminded of this through the training programme of the Department for Education and Employment which they will have undertaken during the 1998 academic year.

The Caper scheme with its step-by-step approach to establishing an effective home–school partnership can be readily applied within the Literacy Hour framework and the first vital step is to develop a school policy which states the school's commitment to the home–school partnership and how this will be enacted. Someone in school should be given the overall responsibility for drawing the threads together and undertaking the necessary steps which we spell out in this book to get the scheme up and going.

The easiest part of the project is getting everybody to agree that it is a good idea. The challenge is to secure a longer-term change in the attitude and practice of teachers and parents. For parents, the change occurs through the support, advice and monitoring provided by school, and for teachers with the realisation that the project generates substantial sustained additional listening time for each child.

The process of change begins with the initial parent and teacher consultation and the parent meetings, all of which we describe in this book.

The profile of the Caper programme in Table 15.1 demonstrates just how important it is to refresh the scheme during its two-and-a-half term duration by feeding in maintenance activity, without which the scheme will rapidly lose its initial impetus and interest, and effort fade. 'Involvement' is a tender plant that needs careful nurturing.

Table 15.1   Maintaining momentum

Project Activities	Introductory	Maintenance	Developmental
First meeting with staff	*		
First meeting with parents	*		
Staff discussion	*		
Caper Daily Comment Booklet		*	
Sending books home		*	
Parent booklet	*	*	
Workshops		*	*
Caper clinics		*	*
Poster competition, etc.		*	
Parent questionnaires		*	*
Newsletters	*		
Publicity	*		
Displays and exhibitions		*	
Reports to school governors	*	*	*
School based research		*	*

The Caper clinic and parent workshop materials develop teachers' as well as parents' thinking about how children learn to read. We emphasise in the text that the learning which occurs is of a two-way nature and that school practice will also be modified through work with parents. Involving parents at the planning stage of a project helps to guarantee its success, but a feedback loop to the project needs to be firmly established so that parents' views are seen to be taken on board. The very partnership which the project establishes acts back on the project itself and helps to sustain it.

Caper reminds all involved that reading is first and foremost *fun*. Caper is *not* about helping children to progress more rapidly through their class reading scheme, which is firmly established in parents and children's minds as *work*. Caper is attempting to re-emphasise to parents and children that books can be a source of fun, magic and mystery.

Caper is very firmly based in children's fiction and sees the reader as one who is constantly engaged in constructing meanings from texts. The parental role is to facilitate this process by encouraging the child to make sense of what is being read.

Parents are constantly reminded in the scheme that they should enjoy reading with their children and should not treat reading as an obstacle race in which it is almost necessary to fail in order to succeed. An extensive range of strategies is suggested which parents can encourage their children to use. Caper attempts to meet parents' anxiety that children will not learn to read through enjoyment.

Children's perception of reading is almost certainly influenced by the methods which schools employ to teach it and most children in the early years believe that there is a set of skills to be learnt before reading can occur. Reading equals work, equals competition and equals failure for some and success for others. The emphasis in this scheme upon parents as facilitators and as adults who model the pleasure to be had from books comes as a welcome relief at home.

A significant proportion of pupils reject easy books that they can read in favour of hard books that they have difficulty in reading. Similarly, they reject 'thin' books in favour of 'thick' books because they are being led to the view that the 'good' reader naturally gravitates towards the thicker book! This is the message which the school's reading scheme inevitably carries and is another example of how texts teach what readers learn (Meek 1988).

Easy-to-read texts, which may be complex in structure, are strongly recommended for Caper because they enable children to practise being readers. They contain the necessary elements: familiar and new vocabulary, repetition of themes and vocabulary *and* a sustained interest level – a story which engages in ways that we do not always understand (but which children want to hear again and again), and written language which accords with a given set of rules. The books themselves teach reading. We are persuaded that behaving like a reader helps you to become one (Smith 1986).

Caper attempts to encourage a creative and imaginative response to reading from children, by getting parents to model enjoyment and to share this. Therefore we do *not* count the number of pages that a parent and child read together and limit the session spent on reading to not more than 20 minutes. This makes the necessary allowance for individual differences, which reading a set number of pages may not. Furthermore, timed support is appreciated by parents who will know exactly what is expected of them.

We emphasis again and again that teachers using Caper need to be constantly looking out for books – a plentiful supply of children's fiction which is good and easy-to-read. A class of 30 pupils will need a book stock of 50 books per half-term. This stock will then have to be changed or swapped every half-term. For the five half-terms of the scheme, approximately 250 books are therefore required for the class. Do not be put off if there are not enough books or enough easy books to start with. Aim to build up the stock as the scheme goes on. We have suggested ways of doing this, either through borrowing books via a local resources or teachers' centre, through the schools' library service or through the schools' parent–teacher association. Learning to read with insufficient books is like learning to cycle without a bike, and about as useful.

Nearly every school would claim to *involve* parents. Our contention is that the word covers a wide range of practice and in some schools the home–school reading scheme operates in name only. Teachers pay lip service to it, with the result that the substantial gains that parent support makes possible are only partially realised.

Research has demonstrated unequivocally that, where staff are committed to a scheme, where a policy is in place that is owned by staff, parents and children, where a full range of maintenance activities are built in and the necessary materials are available, substantial gains can be made in children's reading skills through a home–school reading project.

This book, based upon the successful experience of the many teachers we have worked with in England and Wales, can help to ensure that every school can mount and sustain an effective reading partnership with the wider community.

Appendices

Daily Comment Booklet (pp. 115–18)

This is an absolutely essential element of the scheme. Either use this booklet or produce a modified version. The Caper Comment Booklet assumes that parents will read with their children each evening. Parents are quite willing to make this level of commitment.

Remember to 'personalise' the booklet by printing the name of your class or school on the cover. Try to make your booklet attractive and professional in appearance. A loose sheet of paper will not give the scheme the best kind of image in children's and parents' eyes.

Instructions for assembling the Daily Comment Booklet

Reproduce the four pages which comprise the Comment Booklet, fold along the dashed lines and photocopy back to back. Insert the pages of ruled lines within the cover pages and staple the booklet together.

Caper Guidance Booklet (pp. 119–24)

This is the handout given to parents at the initial meeting. It should be personalised with the name of your class or school. It should be modified for the parents of younger nursery or reception class pupils.

The Guidance Booklet is a worthwhile investment and you are strongly advised to produce one along the lines indicated. The Caper Guidance Booklet helps to remind parents what was said in the meeting and will be used by parents to explain to other potential helpers at home, unable to attend, what went on.

Instructions for assembling the Caper Guidance Booklet

Reproduce the six pages which comprise the Caper Guidance Booklet, fold along the dashed lines and stick together in pairs, back to back. Assemble the booklet by following the numbering of the pages. (Note that Humpty Dumpty forms the centre of the booklet.)

Name of School

The

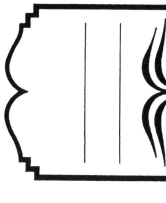

Daily Comment Booklet

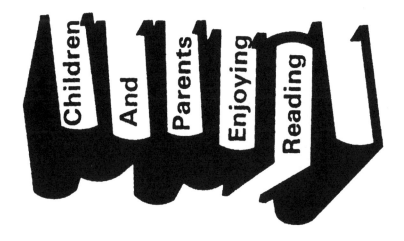

Children
And
Parents
Enjoying
Reading

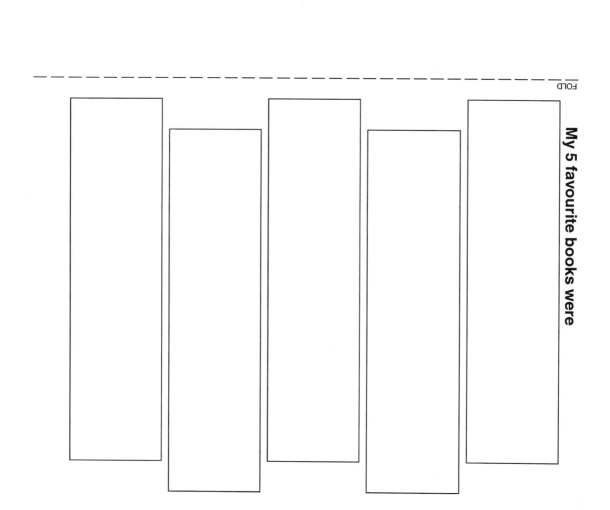

FOLD

My 5 favourite books were

Week	Your comments	Teacher
1 M		
T		
W		
Th		
F		
w/e		
2 M		
T		
W		
Th		
F		
w/e		
3 M		
T		
W		
Th		
F		
w/e		
Teacher's comments		

FOLD -

Week	Your comments	Teacher
10 M		
T		
W		
Th		
F		
w/e		
11 M		
T		
W		
Th		
F		
w/e		
12 M		
T		
W		
Th		
F		
w/e		
Teacher's comments		

Week		Your comments						Teacher
4	M							
	T							
	W							
	Th							
	F							
	w/e							
5	M							
	T							
	W							
	Th							
	F							
	w/e							
6	M							
	T							
	W							
	Th							
	F							
	w/e							

Teacher's comments

FOLD

Week		Your comments						Teacher
7	M							
	T							
	W							
	Th							
	F							
	w/e							
8	M							
	T							
	W							
	Th							
	F							
	w/e							
9	M							
	T							
	W							
	Th							
	F							
	w/e							

Teacher's comments

Scoring key

If you answered 'Yes' to the questions, score the following:

1, one; 2, one; 3, one; 4, one; 5, three; 6(a), one; 6(b), zero; 6(c), zero; 6(d), two; 7, one; 8, zero; 9, one; 10, one; 11, four; 12, three

How did you make out?

Score		
16–20	Excellent. You should have no difficulty in helping your child.	
10–16	Very good.	
4–10	Only average. Room for improvement here!	
0–4	Not too good. Follow the advice in the book and take the test again in 2 or 3 months.	

The Caper Guidance Booklet

Helping your child to enjoy reading

School:

Test yourself

Put a circle around Yes or No.

1. I have talked to my child about the book that we are reading.   Yes/No
2. I have read the story book myself.   Yes/No
3. My child can tell me what comes next in the story.   Yes/No
4. My child can tell the story in his or her own words.   Yes/No
5. We read together every night.   Yes/No
6. When my child comes to an unfamiliar word I: Yes/No

    (a) give it straight away   Yes/No
    (b) sound it out   Yes/No
    (c) make him or her sound it out   Yes/No
    (d) help him to guess sensibly   Yes/No

7. My child belongs to and visits the local library.   Yes/No
8. Helping with reading is left to Mum.   Yes/No
9. Before buying a book for my child I read it myself where possible.   Yes/No
10. I like books myself.   Yes/No
11. I can name four children's authors.   Yes/No
12. I am confident my child will be a successful reader.   Yes/No

Parents often ask themselves, 'How can I help my child read?'

Many are afraid to help in case they interfere with the school's reading approach.

Yet 60% of parents help their children to learn to read.

Other sources of books

Books can be borrowed through our local library. Ask the Librarian's advice. It is helpful if you know the author or title of the books your child likes.

Bookshops

Remember when you buy books to buy those that your children like and not the books that *you* think they *ought* to read. There is no point in forcing them to read books they do not enjoy or understand.

FOLD

10

Reading is

fun

exciting

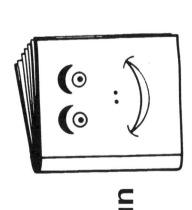

essential

3

Your children will always have a book from school at home.

They will have a termly booklet for you to comment in each day.

Use the booklet to record their reading and any problems that you discover.

Week		Your comments	Teacher
1	M	He read well; the story flowed.	
	T	Keeps reading 'saw' for 'was'.	
	W	We are both excited by this adventure.	
	Th	Both of us too tired after the supermarket.	

FOLD

TALKING AND READING

You taught him to talk.

He listened to you. You listened to him in turn.

Then you shared conversations.

We can apply this to reading.

First, read to your child.

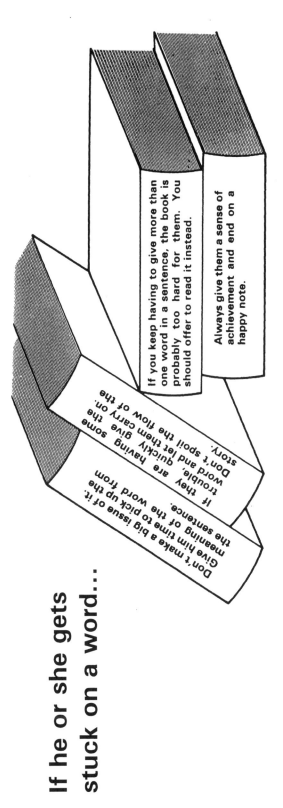

If he or she gets stuck on a word…

Don't make a big issue of it. Give him time to pick up the meaning of the word from the sentence.

If they are having some trouble, quickly give the word and let them carry on. Don't spoil the flow of the story.

If you keep having to give more than one word in a sentence, the book is probably too hard for them. You should offer to read it instead.

Always give them a sense of achievement and end on a happy note.

and share a book.

Then, listen to your child read,

READING TOGETHER

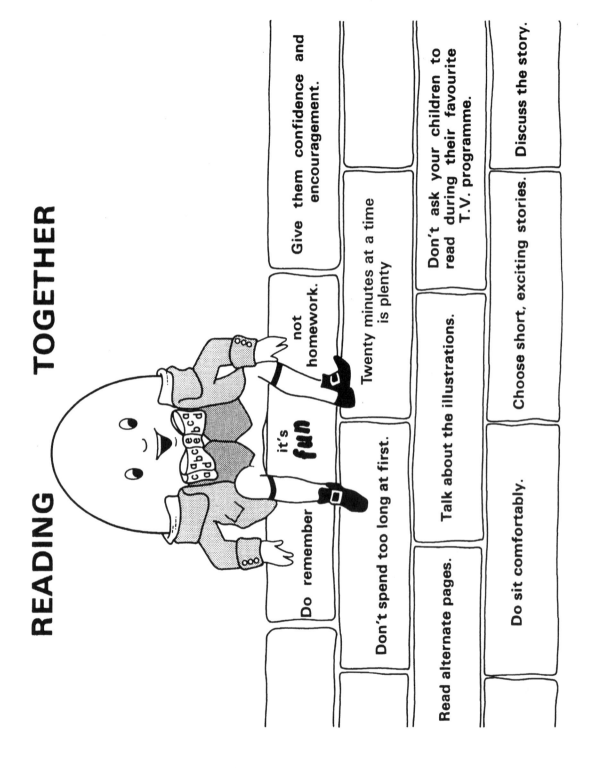

Do remember it's **fun** not homework.

Give them confidence and encouragement.

Twenty minutes at a time is plenty

Don't spend too long at first.

Don't ask your children to read during their favourite T.V. programme.

Talk about the illustrations.

Read alternate pages.

Choose short, exciting stories.

Discuss the story.

Do sit comfortably.

Parent Questionnaires 1 and 2

These are the questionnaires used in the Caper scheme so far. Parent Questionnaire 1 is used after half-term of term one, and Parent Questionnaire 2 early in term two. They provide a guide to the level of parental support given to the scheme; they also serve as a reminder to parents that the scheme is still very much underway.

Give them a try, modified for your own use. The response to the questionnaires is both encouraging and instructive.

Examples are given in Figures A.1 and A.2 and may be photocopied freely.

Children's attitude scales

Girls' Attitude Scale 1 (Figure A.3), Boys' Attitude Scale 1 (Figure A.4), Children's Attitude Scale 2 (Figure A.5), Girls' Attitude Scale 3 (Figures A.6) and Boys' Attitude Scale 3 (Figure A.7) are given below.

These are easy to construct and test out. The results can be very helpful, both in terms of what they reveal about an individual child and about how attitudes may be changing over time.

Attitude Scale 1 has been used successfully with six- to seven-year-olds but would need to be modified for use with children younger than that. Attitude Scale 2 can also be used with six- to eight-year olds.

Attitude Scale 3 is more suited to children who are eight or older.

Mark all the scales by awarding one point for each positive comment. Make a note of each child's total score and compare this with the score that the child obtains when reassessed.

Parent Questionnaire 1

Child's Name _____ Class _____

1. Did you attend one of the reading meetings? Yes/No

2. Have you received a copy of the Caper Guidance Booklet? Yes/No

3. Does your son or daughter have a school reading book at home?
   Constantly _____ Occasionally _____ Rarely _____ Never _____

4. Do you hear him or her read from this book? Yes/No

5. If so, how often?
   Daily _____ Every other day _____ Twice a week _____ Less often _____

6. When you hear your child read, how long does the session last?
   5 min _____ 10 min _____ 15 min _____ 20 min _____ longer _____

7. Does anyone else hear him or her read?
   Mother _____ Father _____ Grandparent _____
   Others (please specify) _____

8. What is your child's attitude to these sessions?
   Eager to read _____ Unwilling _____ Reluctant to read _____
   Refuses _____ Willing to read _____

9. How often does your child change their reading book?
   Weekly _____ Fortnightly _____ Monthly _____ Each Half Term _____

10. Do you complete the daily Comment Booklet? Yes/No

11. Are the books always easy for him/her to read? Yes/No
    If not, what do you do?
    Read it myself ____ Read it first ____ Let him struggle ____ Return it ___

12. Other than school, does your child have books from other sources?
    If yes, where from? Yes/No
    _____
    _____

13. Have you made contact with teachers in the school regarding your child's reading since the scheme began? Yes/No

14. What, if any, have been the benefits of this scheme?
    _____
    _____
    _____

Signed _____ Mother/Father/Guardian

Figure A.1 Parent Questionnaire 1

Parent Questionnaire 2

Dear Parent,

In order to help us to follow the reading project's progress, could you please fill in the questionnaire below and send it back to school as soon as possible.

Many thanks in anticipation of your cooperation.

1. How often does your child have a book home from school?
   Rarely _____ Never _____ Constantly _____ Occasionally ____

2. How often do you listen to your child read?
   Twice a week ____ Daily ____ Every other day ___ Less often ___

3. How long do you listen for?
   20 min ____ 5 min _____ 15 min ____ 25 min ____ 10 min _____

4. Who else listens to your child read?
   Mother ____ Father _____ Grandparent _____ Brother, Sister ____
   Others (please specify) _____

5. How would you describe your child's attitude to reading aloud to you?
   Hesitant __ Willing ___ Unwilling _ Eager to read ___ Refuses __

6. How often do you make a comment in his or her Comment Booklet?
   Twice a week ____ Daily ____ Every other day ___ Less often ___

Signed _____ Parent of _____

Figure A.2 Parent Questionnaire 2

Girls' Attitude Scale 1

Name: _____ School: _____

Class: _____

Helen is a little girl. She comes to school every day, except for weekends and holidays, of course!

Put a tick by the right face

1. How does Helen feel when her parent says, 'Read this story out loud to me'?

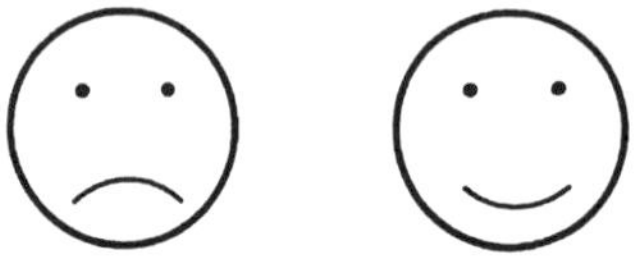

2. How does Helen feel about reading at home?

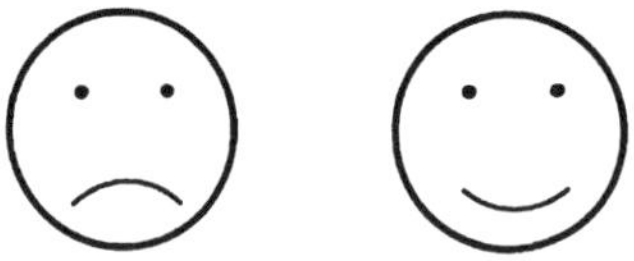

3. How does Helen feel about reading to her teacher at school?

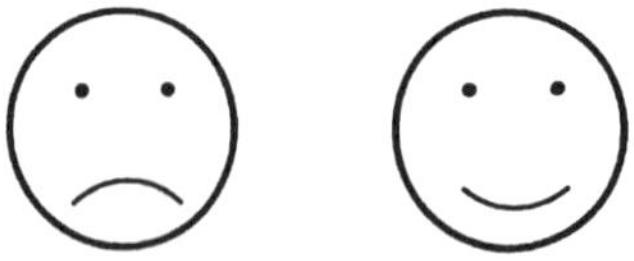

4. How does Helen feel when her parent or her teacher reads a story out loud to her?

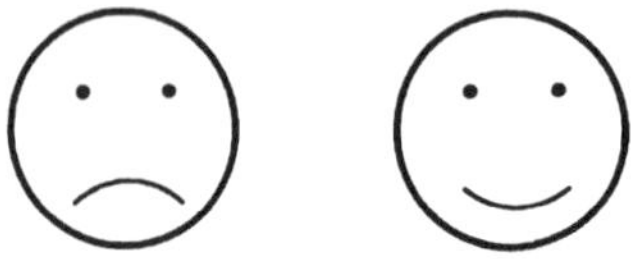

5. How does Helen feel when she reads to herself (for instance, in bed)?

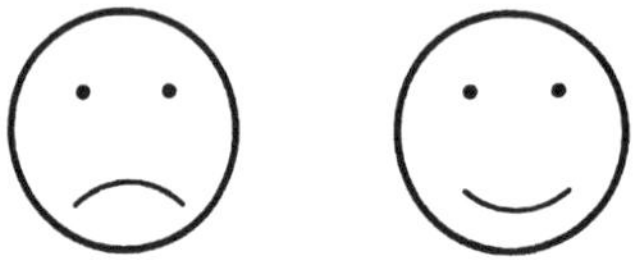

Figure A.3 Girls' Attitude Scale 1

Boys' Attitude Scale 1

Name: _____ School: _____

Class: _____

Peter is a little boy. He comes to school every day, except weekends and holidays, of course!

Put a tick by the right face.

1. How does Peter feel when his parent says, 'Read this story out loud to me'?

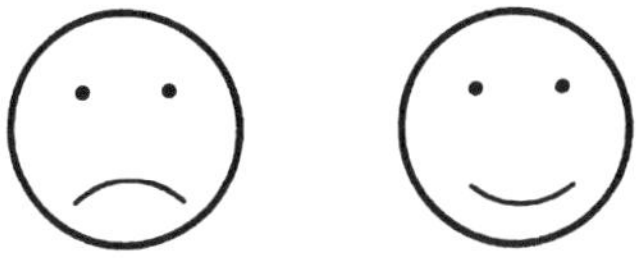

2. How does Peter feel about reading at home?

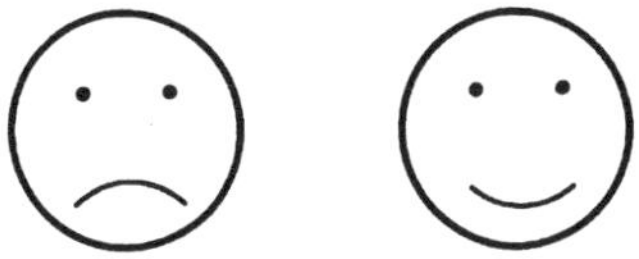

3. How does Peter feel about reading to his teacher at school?

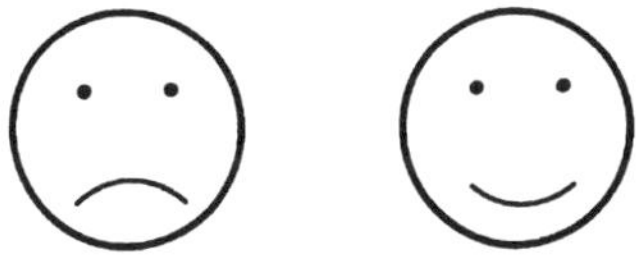

4. How does Peter feel when his parent or his teacher reads a story out loud to him?

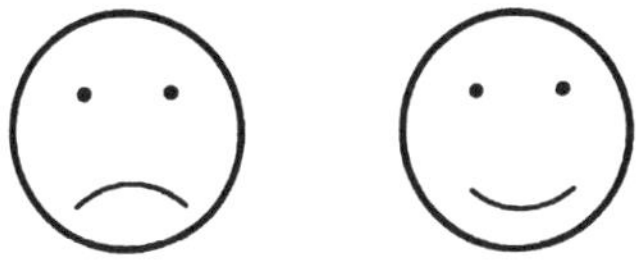

5. How does Peter feel when he reads to himself (for instance, in bed)?

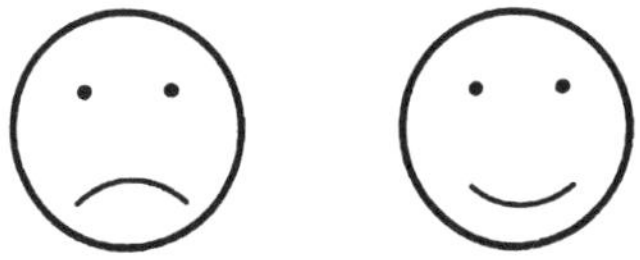

Figure A.4 Boys' Attitude Scale 1

Children's Attitude Scale 2

Put a circle around Yes or No.

1. Do you like reading books out loud to your mother?   Yes/No

2. Do you like reading at home?   Yes/No

3. Do you like reading at school?   Yes/No

4. When your parent asks you to read, do you pretend not to hear?   Yes/No

5. When your parent or your teacher read a story out loud, is that the only time that you like books?   Yes/No

6. When your parent asks you to read, do you sometimes get cross?   Yes/No

7. Are you always reading books?   Yes/No

8. Have you read so many books that you can't remember them all?   Yes/No

9. Do you always tell your parent about the story you're reading?   Yes/No

10. Do you like reading to yourself, especially in bed, best of all?   Yes/No

The best sort of books are _____

_____

_____

_____

The worst sort of books are _____

_____

_____

_____

Figure A.5 Childrens' Attitude Scale 2

Boys' Attitude Scale 3

Name: _____ School: _____

Class: _____

Peter did not like reading books out loud to his parent (like me/not like me). He did not like reading at home (like me/not like me) and he did not enjoy reading at school (like me/not like me).

If his parent asked him to read to him or her, he would pretend not to hear (like me/not like me), or sometimes he would even get cross (like me/not like me).

The only time that he liked books was when his parent or his teacher read a story out loud (like me/not like me).

His brother David was always reading books (like me/not like me). David had read so many books that he could not remember them all (like me/not like me).

David always told his parent about the story that he was reading (like me/not like me). He would ask them to listen to him read.

Best of all David liked to read to himself, especially in bed (like me/not like me).

The best sorts of books are _____

_____

_____

_____

The worst sort of books are _____

_____

_____

_____

_____

Figure A.6 Boys' Attitude Scale 2

Girls' Attitude Scale 3

Name: _____   School: _____

Class: _____

Helen did not like reading books out loud to her parent (like me/not like me). She did not like reading at home (like me/not like me) and she did not enjoy reading at school (like me/not like me).

If her parent asked Helen to read to him or her, she would pretend not to hear (like me/not like me), or sometimes she would even get cross (like me/not like me).

The only time that she liked books was when her parent or her teacher read a story out loud (like me/not like me).

Her sister Mandy was always reading books (like me/not like me). Mandy had read so many books that she could not remember them all (like me/not like me).

Mandy always told her parent about the story that she was reading (like me/not like me). She would ask them to listen to her read.

Best of all Mandy liked to read to herself, especially in bed (like me/not like me).

The best sort of books are _____

_____

_____

_____

_____

The worst sort of books are _____

_____

_____

_____

_____

Figure A.7 Girls' Attitude Scale 3

References

Andrew, P. and Provis, W. M. (1983) 'One school's experience in setting up a scheme to involve parents in listening to their children read', *Links*, Autumn, 26–9.

Atkin, J. and Bastiani, J. (1985) *A Survey of Initial Training*. Nottingham: University of Nottingham.

Bastiani, J.(1993) *UK Directory of Home–School Initiatives*, 2nd edn. London: Royal Society of Arts.

Bastiani, J. and Wolfendale, S. (1996) *Home–School Work in Britain*. London: David Fulton Publishers.

Bettleheim, B. and Zelan, K. (1982) *On Learning to Read: The Child's Fascination with Meaning*. London: Thames and Hudson.

Branston, P. and Provis, W. M. (1984) *Caper: A Resource Pack for West Glamorgan Schools*. Swansea: West Glamorgan County Council.

Branston, P. (1988) 'Reading: it's all in the mind', in Reid, K. (ed.) *Troubled Children*. Oxford: Blackwell.

Branston, P. (1996) 'Children and parents enjoying reading', in Wolfendale, S. and Topping, K. (eds) *Family Involvement in Literacy*. London: Cassell.

Bushell, R., Miller, A. and Robson, D. (1982) 'Parents as remedial teachers', *Association of Educational Psychologists Journal* **5**(9), 7–13.

Clay, M. M. (1979) *Reading: The Patterning of Complex Behaviour*. London: Heinemann.

Curran, P. (1985) 'Parental involvement with nursery aged pupils', Unpublished MEd thesis, University College Swansea.

Davie, R., Goldstein, H. and Butler, N. (1972) *From Birth to Seven*. London: Longman.

Department for Education (1995) *Key Stages 1 and 2 of the National Curriculum*. London: Department for Education.

Department for Education and Employment (1997) *Results of the 1997 National Curriculum Assessments of 11 Year Olds in England*. London: Department for Education and Employment.

Department for Education and Employment (1998a) *The National Project for Literacy and Numeracy*. London: Department for Education and Employment.

Department for Education and Employment (1998b) *The National Literacy Strategy – Framework for Teaching*. London: Department for Education and Employment.

Department for Education and Employment (1998c) *The National Literacy Strategy – The Management of Literacy at School Level*. London: Department for Education and Employment.

Douglas, J. W. B. (1964) *The Home and the School*. London: MacGibbon and Kee.

Edwards, L. and Branston, P. (1979) *Reading, How Parents can Help*. Swansea: West Glamorgan County Council.

Friend, P. (1983) 'Reading and the parent, after the Haringey Reading Project.' *Reading*, **17**, 7–12.

Glynn, T., McNaughton, S., Robinson, V. and Quinn, M. (1979) *Remedial Reading at Home: Helping You Help Your Child*. Wellington, New Zealand: Council for Education Research.

Gregory, E. (1996) 'Learning from the community: a family literacy project with Bangladeshi-origin children in London', in Wolfendale, S. and Topping, K. (eds) *Family Involvement in Literacy*. London: Cassell.

Griffiths, A. and Hamilton, D. (1984) *Parents, Teacher, Child*. London: Methuen.

Hancock, R. and Gale, S. (1992) *The 1991 PACT Survey*. London: PACT.

Hewison, J. (1979) 'Home environment and reading attainment. A study of children in a working-class community', Unpublished PhD thesis, University of London.

Kimberley, K., Meek, M. and Miller, J. (eds) (1992) *New Readings: Contributions to an Understanding of Literacy*. London: A. & C. Black.

Lake, M. (1992) 'Social background and academic performance: evidence from Buckinghamshire', In Pumfrey, P. D. (ed.) *Reading Standards: Issues and Evidence*. Leicester: Division of Educational and Child Psychology, The British Psychological Society.

Lewis, D. (1992) 'Looking for Julius: two children and a picture book', in Kimberley, K., Meek, M. and Miller, J. (eds) *New Readings: Contributions to an Understanding of Literacy*. London: A. & C. Black.

Medcalf, J. and Glynn, T. (1987) 'Assisting teachers to implement peer-tutored remedial reading using pause, prompt and praise procedures. *Queensland Journal of Guidance and Counselling* **1**, 11–23.

Meek, M. (1988) *How Texts Teach What Readers Learn*. Stroud: Thimble Press.

Morgan, R. and Lyon, E. (1979) 'Paired reading: a preliminary report on a technique for parental tuition of reading retarded children', *Journal of Child Psychology and Psychiatry* **20**, 151–60.

Morgan, R.T.T. (1976) 'Paired reading tuition: a preliminary report on a technique for cases of reading deficit', *Child Care, Health and Development* **2**, 13–28.

Payton, S. (1984) *Developing Awareness of Print: A Young Child's First Steps towards Literacy*. *Educational Review Occasional Publications*, No. 2. Birmingham: University of Birmingham.

Provis, W. M. (1983) *Caper – An Interim Report*. Swansea: West Glamorgan County Council.

Smith, F. (1986) *Reading*. Cambridge: Cambridge University Press.

Southgate, V. *et al.* (1981) *Extending Beginning Reading*. London: Heinemann.

Topping, K. J. (1995) *Paired Reading, Spelling and Writing: The Handbook for Parents and Teachers*. London: Cassell.

Topping K. J. and Wolfendale S. (eds) (1985) *Parental Involvement in Children's Reading*. Beckenham: Croom Helm. New York: Nichols.

Tizard, J., Schofield, W. and Hewison, J. (1982) 'Collaboration between teachers and parents in assisting children's reading', *British Journal of Educational Psychology*, **52**, 1–15.

Tucker, N. (1984) *The Child and the Book: a Psychological and Literary Exploration*. Cambridge: Cambridge University Press

Wade, B. (1984) *Story at Home and School*. *Educational Review Occasional Publications*, No. 10. Birmingham: University of Birmingham.

Welsh Office (1987) *The Effects of Parental Involvement in the Development of Reading and Language Skills of Nursery Aged Children*. Cardiff: HMSO.

Wheldall, K., Wenban-Smith, J., Morgan, A. and Quance, B. (1992) 'Reading: how do teachers typically tutor?' *Educational Psychology* **12**, 177–94.

Wheldall, K. and Glynn, T. (1989) *Effective Classroom Learning*. Oxford: Basil Blackwell.

Wolfendale, S. (1992) *Empowering Parents and Teachers: Working for Children*. London: Cassell.

Wolfendale, S. and Topping, K. (eds) (1996) *Family Involvement in Literacy*. London: Cassell.

Index

Comments from parents on the Caper scheme

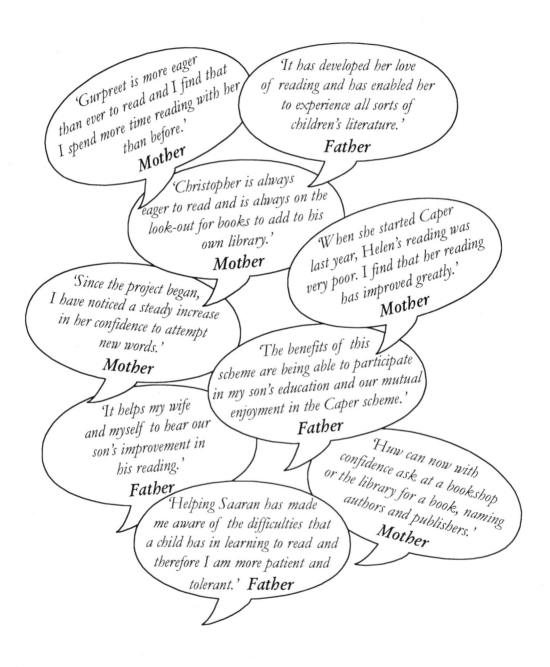